The Super Sprinter's Handbook

How any swimmer can go from Good to Great to Gold!

By Kurt Schallitz

Published By:
Science Based Swimming, LTD.
Livermore, CA

ISBN: 978-1-10505-167-8

First Printing: 2013

5 4 3 2

Dedicated to all of those potential elite athletes that are now or will in the future think of quitting the sport because they didn't *believe* they had what it takes.

AUTHOR'S NOTE

Most of what you have been taught about swimming, most likely, is inaccurate. Most of what you will learn in this book is also most likely to eventually become outdated. So why would you bother to read this book? Because if you are like most swimmers, much of what you have learned over the years was taught to you based on faith in a process that has little, or in some cases no, scientific basis. Everything presented in this book is based and founded in the sciences of math, physics and kinesiology. The wonderful thing about science is that it admits upfront that it is incomplete. Science will never try to offer you the complete solution because it knows that as humans we are not perfect and therefore our understanding of the universe is constantly changing.

As a result, this book does not hope to present itself as an end point for your swimming questions, but rather as a beginning. This is a place to explore new ideas that are based on the best information we have at this time, founded in solid principles of math, science and physics, keeping in mind that some of this information may change over time. It is a book that will improve your swimming because everything in here quite simply works – and it works because it has to work – whether you believe in it or not. That is the power of science, and that is a very good point to start relearning what we *think* we already know about this sport we call swimming.

- Coach X

INTRODUCTION

This book is the compilation of years of work, not just by the author, but by uncountable numbers of scientists and coaches from around the world. For those that took their time to read early versions of this book and provide feedback, I will be forever grateful. It was the feedback of regular age group swimmers from across the United States, and from countries like Mexico, El Salvador, Curacao, Aruba, England, Australia, Panama, the Netherlands and Canada that helped to shape this book. In a real sense this is a book by swimmers for swimmers as much as it is a book by scientists for swimmers.

For those that know me or who have taken part in one of my clinics, you will know that I absolutely love to bring science to the masses. In my clinics I try to deliver the science content in a fun and exciting way that swimmers of all ages can understand. During clinics I do experiments to demonstrate wake forces by sucking an egg into a bottle; demonstrate buoyancy with a scale, a magic penny and a beaker of water; demonstrate form drag with an exploding beach ball, and always open a clinic with a mentalist trick to warn swimmers against pseudo-science. To me art is as much a part of science as science is a part of swimming. The two are inseparable.

When I first sat down to write this book, it was my intention to footnote each and every sentence with supporting studies and links to scientific journals to support each statement. Each week, I read between one to five books or research papers. I have gathered a massive library of data to support the principles that I write about in these pages. As a person of science, my natural tendency when writing is to document, document, and document. However, when early versions of this book were sent to swimmers for review, the very clear and consistent feedback was: drop the footnotes!

This feedback came hard to me. It went against almost all that I believe in. But when I talked with the reviewers it became clear that they had picked up on the science without ever having the need to refer to a single footnoted study, research paper or diagram. Eventually I gave in and produced a copy of the book free of all references and footnotes. This I sent to a new set of reviewers, fully expecting to be blasted for not supporting the ideas. Instead, the feedback was astonishingly positive and the book remains footnote free.

In place of the footnotes I instead added simple experiments that any swimmer could do to prove to themself how a given concept worked, and beyond that, how it affected them directly. These experiments are denoted throughout the book with an icon of a swimming suit in the margin. After receiving feedback on this new version of the book, I knew that the original reviewers had been correct. The text reads much smoother, and is several pages shorter after having removed the references.

During the second round of review, one swimmer mentioned to me that he particularly enjoyed how I would tell stories about real swimmers during my clinics and suggested that perhaps I could add some of those stories in the book. It was from here that the story about hunting night crawlers for fun and profit came into the book. Soon many more swimmers wrote in with their own stories to share. In the end, I decided to go with stories that I played witness to. It was the only way I could ensure the details were accurate. However, I decided to change the names of the participants in all of the stories. In so doing I decided to use the names of swimmers who had submitted their own stories, which I did not use. In this way, they get mention in the book even if the stories associated with their names are not actually their own.

Lastly I wanted to acknowledge that this book is only a beginning. There was simply so much information that I wanted to share that at one point, this "handbook" was nearly 500 pages! In fact, it wasn't getting any smaller either. Fortunately I met a great personal coach, Tom, who helped me to work on my skill of resolving my ideas. If not for Tom and his organization, this book never would have been completed. To him and the people at A *n Appropriate Response*, I owe a great deal of thanks.

Gone from this text are chapters on psychology and nutrition. I have decided to remove the section on drills from this book and put it into an entirely separate book focusing exclusively on when to apply each to help with specific stroke problems. Gone is the chapter on how body suits were bogus until 2007; I even had interviewed a body suit manufacturer who went on record and admitted that it was all smoke and mirrors and placebo effect until they added rubber to improve buoyancy – the suits never actually made you swim faster, marketing did. Gone are the chapters showing why jammers are the slowest of all suits and why most swimmers should wear briefs whenever possible. Gone is the study showing why training with drag suits often makes you slower during a race. Instead I focused on the parts of the book that the early reviewers said made the most immediate time impacts for them.

The book has been broken into two main sections. Pre-meet and meet. The pre-meet section covers things like warm-ups, stretching, starts and finishes. The meet portion of the book focuses on each of the four major competitive strokes. It breaks down each into the scientifically relevant parts of each stroke and explains how to significantly drop time in each using very simple techniques.

When I first began to write this book, I was concerned that the information within would be too simplistic. I figured that everyone must know this stuff. But the feedback I received from the swimmers who reviewed the book quickly changed my mind. Everyone raved about how much they learned from the book.

Over the years that I've been working on this book I have also been conducting swimming clinics around the world and also coaching a local team on the side. The one thing I've found most incredible over the years is the change in vocabulary I hear on deck during meets. Only a few years ago, I was the only one on deck shouting "push" during breaststroke while others around me were shouting "pull." I was almost always alone when yelling, "head down" in backstroke or "rotate" and now these words are ubiquitous. For years I was the only one at the meet measuring distance per stroke instead of just measuring stroke rates, today this is no longer the case. Many coaches looked at me when I would videotape each race for my swimmers and review them on the spot after each race and routinely shoot underwater video during practice. Today DVR systems are commonly marketed to coaches for swim practice. I am still one of the few coaches I know who always uses an underwater speaker to provide real-time immediate feedback to swimmers during practice. I suspect that soon, this too will become common.

All of these changes are great to see. I am excited to be publishing my first book. I hope you have as much fun reading it as I have had writing it. Please feel free to share your experience by emailing us at **SBSCSWIM@GMAIL.COM**. If your experience is in anyway close to those who gave their time to help review the early versions of this book, you can expect some amazing results. So sit back, relax, and let's put science to the test. It's time to become a *Super Sprinter!*

A word about credit:

Many people will most likely ask – why do you not use your name? Why go by "Coach X"? If you believe so strongly in these principles, why not identify yourself? So very well, I shall: My name is Coach Kurt Schallitz. I have been coaching for over two decades and I have traveled around the United States and around the world offering technique oriented training camps to swimmers and to coaches. So why go by the moniker of Coach X? Because I do not wish to be the one to take credit for what is presented in this book. What you will find in these pages is based on the work of countless scientists, mathematicians, physicists, sports medicine doctors, coaches and other people with more letters behind their name than exist in some alphabets! While I do have a considerable amount of personal experience and knowledge, I do not wish to even attempt to say that I know what I am talking about unless I can show a scientific study to back up my beliefs, and usually I won't say anything without having two or three studies all in agreement. So, credit is not due to me, but rather to those who have dedicated themselves to finding the solutions for all of us. To them, I give a great salute, and hope that their knowledge and my experiences can help to make your swimming dreams a reality

Coach X

CONTENTS

PRE-RACE 1

    WARMUP 3

    CRAMPS 7

    STRETCHING 9

    PRE-EVENT WARM-UPS 10

    AT THE STARTING BLOCKS 12

PRE-RACE TIP SUMMARY 16

AT THE RACE 17

    STARTS 19

    STREAMLINES 31

    TURNS 41

    FINISHES 51

    STROKE SCIENCE 58

    FRONT CRAWL 66

    BACKSTROKE 104

    BREASTSTROKE 121

    BUTTERFLY 141

PUTTING IT ALL TOGETHER 161

    BALROTELONPROP 161

EPILOG 164

ABOUT THE AUTHOR 167

TABLE OF EXPERIMENTS

PLASTIC MAN 9

DISTANCE PER START 24

STREAMLINES 32

ROTAION AND STREAMLINES...35

DEPTH CHARGES 36

THE SUB ZERO CLUB..43

FEET PLACEMENT FOR TURNS 46

SPINNING CHAIR OF DEATH 47

FAR REACHING 53

SWIMMING BACKWARDS 71

CORDS OF SPEED..77

NON-NEWTONIAN FLUIDS...78

FUN WITH MATH..79

CENTER OF GRAVITY...83

KINETIC CHAIN 87

WHAT ARE YOU LOOKING AT?..88

LESS IS MORE 96

FLAT HEAD 106

LEVERAGE..113

PUSH PULL KICK...121

SEA SLINKY 124

USING A LANE AS A MEASURING STICK 132

NO ARM BUTTERFLY 144

BOOING BUTTERFLY 152

PRE-RACE

WARMUP

"When you make the finding yourself - even if you're the last person on Earth to see the light - you'll never forget it."
Carl Sagan

WARMUP

There you are on the starting block. You are wearing your brand new technical briefs – fast. You look to your left and there is a kid about one full head taller than you. You look to the right and there is another kid in a full body suit (weren't those things banned!) looking like he is two age groups up from yours. For the flick of a second, you panic. As you look around you realize that you are in the center lane – top seed! Yes, you are ready for this. Today, you are going to show everyone what all your practice and hard work was for. Today is your day. You stand poised, ready to go, waiting for the sonic beep on the starter. Waiting, waiting, then...

Beep!

You jump in! Perfect parabolic entry! Perfect streamline - you even remembered to stream line your feet!

Beep!

What? What was that? Another beep? Are they recalling the race? No, it was probably just the starter for the odd heats.

You break the surface with a perfectly balanced body and begin your stroke. Beep!

Hunh? What was that? Well, you're not going to look around; you *know* that you are in first place right now and you're going to stay there.

Beep! Beep! Beep!

The pool slowly disappears from around you and the space is filled with blackness as you open your eyes to find that you are still at home in bed. The beeping sound is from your alarm clock and it is now 5:30 AM! Ugh! Why do you have to get up so early again? The meet doesn't start until 9:00 AM. Oh yeah – warm-ups start at 7:30. Time to get up and get ready.

Have you ever wondered why doing a warm up is so important?

HOLLY'S STORY

Let me introduce you to a swimmer that I know. Her name is Holly and she is nine. During her practices, she almost always beat the other swimmers in her lane; some of whom were much older than her. On Fridays when the team did relays, Holly was always one of the first kids to get picked. All of the kids in Holly's group expected that Holly would soon be moving up to the next group. But day after day, Holly stayed in her group, not moving up. In fact a younger boy who started after Holly even passed right by her into the next group. Holly was the kind of swimmer that really had a lot of potential, but just couldn't prove her times in a swimming meet. It was as if Holly hit a brick wall with her times. She would practice hard every day, but for some reason she simply could not reach an A time at a meet. Holly was becoming frustrated, and so were her

4

parents, not to mention her coach. Fortunately Holly made a discovery that got her all the way from mediocre to the All Stars! What did she do? Here is her story:

While Holly would attend nearly every meet, there was one thing very inconsistent about her. Nobody ever knew when she would show up! Most of the time she would appear only about one hour before her first event of the day. Holly said the reason for her late arrival was that her parents were lazy and did not want to drag the family to a swim meet only to sit around and wait several hours for the first event. But even if that was the case, Holly should have told her family how important it is to get to the meet early and why.

The coach on Holly's team was getting very frustrated. Several hours after the team had finished warm up, Holly would first arrive. She would have no time to get in the pool and do the team's general warm up. In fact, she didn't even want to warm up before her events. Holly said this would tire her out and that she would not have any energy left for her race.

Yet at every meet, Holly swam a good race. The problem was, she never swam a *great* race! Because of her lack of warm up, Holly faced many problems in the pool. Her dives were awful; she often had very poor turns and looked like a pinball going down the lanes. Finally the coach decided to speak with Holly's parents about getting to the meet earlier. When he did, he received a lot of resistance from Holly's parents. They explained that they have two other children, both in different sports and they could not get Holly to her swimming meet any earlier. Even still the parents were blaming the coach for Holly's performance at her meets. The parents wanted better results. Finally the coach simply said that Holly would have to swim for a different team. That was harsh! But the parent's finally realized how important it was to arrive early and allow Holly enough time to do the warm up.

At the next meet Holly's parents decided to take some of the team tents so that they would have to arrive early and set them up. As it turns out, it wasn't just the parents that had a problem with a morning warm-up. Holly complained that the warm-up was making her tired. In fact she even cried to the coach that she just didn't want to do it. Fortunately Holly's coach did not give in. He made her get in the water and do the general warm up with the rest of the team. Once Holly's first event was getting closer, the coach asked her to again get in the water and do a very short warm-up specific to her stroke. Again Holly cried to her parents that the warm-up would make her tired and that she would get an awful time.

As it turns out, Holly did get an awful time on each of her races that day. Most likely it was not due to the warm-up, but rather in spite of it. Holly was trying to do poorly so that the coach would not want her to do a warm-up at the meets any more. To solve this problem, her coach increased the yardage during regular practice to ensure that she would no longer get tired at the meets.

Finally Holly got the message. At the next meet, she arrived early and did the team warm-up without any complaints. She also did the pre-race warm-up as instructed.

After about three meets, something amazing happened. Holly's times began to drop; all of them. Significantly. Her parents were thrilled. Suddenly the girl that could never get an A time was walking around with enough medals around her neck to look like a young rap star. But it didn't stop there. Only four meets after making a warm-up part of her routine, Holly received six new Junior Olympic times in a single meet! Before turning ten, Holly qualified for the All Star meet in her United States Swimming section. An incredible achievement all made possible simply by a morning warm-up followed by an event specific warm up before each race.

How did such a simple thing as a warm-up accomplish all of that? Let's take a look.

MUSCLE FATIGUE
OR HOW TO CATCH NIGHT CRAWLERS FOR FUN AND PROFIT.

Okay, it may seem like a story about catching night crawlers would be out of place in a book on swimming, but just read on and if you don't see the connection, at least you will be able to setup a nice side business and open a bait shop. When Coach X was younger he really liked to go fishing. There was a river near his house that was home to several small mouth bass that seemed to bite on nothing but night crawlers (that's worms for those who don't know). The problem was that Coach X was very young and didn't have enough money to go out and buy night crawlers each time he wanted to go fishing.

Fortunately, even at a very young age, Coach X was still Mr. Science. He did a lot of research on Earth worms and made some amazing discoveries. Oh and by the way, we didn't have the Internet back then, so imagine a ten year old kid going to the library and reading books just to get worms to fish with!

The first thing you need to know about catching worms is that you should wet the ground thoroughly during the day. At night when you go out to hunt, use a bright flashlight, but cover it with orange or red cellophane. It turns out that worms can't see that color of light and so they will never know you are coming! If you don't, as soon the light hits them they will quickly slink back into their hole and you'll never catch one. So far, so good. Now you can stealthily walk around your yard searching for worms near the surface. The problem is that most worms are still half way in their holes. When you try to grab them and tug on them they break in half and you have a dead worm that the fish won't bite.

For a while this caused a lot of problems for young Coach X. So it was back to the library. After doing even more research he found that Earth worms have muscles just like people do. And that is why they can tug with such force to get back into their holes. He also found out that it takes a chemical called ATP to make muscles work and that worms use up all of theirs in about 15 seconds. Armed with this knowledge, Coach X went out the next night and not a single worm got away. The trick – simply hold the worm for 15 seconds without pulling on it and it will go completely limp. It can't crawl back into its hole. Then all you need to do is pick it up and put it in your bucket!

So now you know the secret to hunting night crawlers. And what does any of that have to do with swimming? I'm sure some of you have already figured it out. Just like the worms, you use the same chemicals to make your muscles work. By doing the right things before your race you can make the muscles work very, very well. If you do the wrong things, your muscles will be just like that limp flabby worm. How can we treat our muscles well and increase our efficiency? Read on *Super Sprinter*!

ZERO TO 60 MPH IN 2.0 SECONDS

There is a reason that we call a warm-up a warm-up. It is because that is literally what you are doing with your muscles. Your muscles are made up of several different kinds of fibers and tissues. Those fibers and tissues all require oxygen from the blood, energy and chemicals to work properly. When you first start to use your muscles, they will make use of the energy that they already have lying around in the cells. The problem comes when that fuel and chemical storage begins to runs out.

Think of it like this: Imagine that you have an event at 11:30 am. You have arrived at the pool around 9:00 am and you missed the team's general warm-up. You have decided that you don't want to do a stroke specific warm-up before your event. Now two and a half hours later you stand up on the starting block. All day the activity level of your muscles has been about zero. The starter sounds. At that moment your poor body has to go from 0 miles per hour to maximum speed in about two seconds. Not even a top of the line sports car can do that! Yet for some reason you think your body can? Well, if this thought experiment describes you, then I have news for you: It Can't!

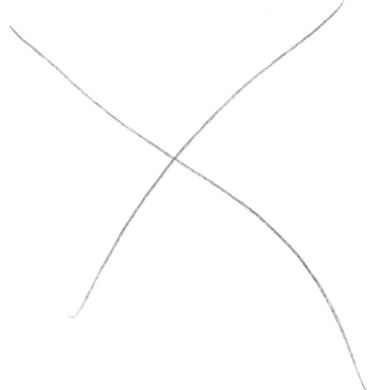

YOUR HIGH POWERED, REVVED UP, BODY MACHINE

Your body is very efficient at creating energy from the foods you eat. Normally, it breaks down the food with oxygen to produce fuel that your muscles can use (Aerobic Respiration). When you warm up, you increase your heart rate and take in more oxygen. That oxygen flows from your lungs into your blood which then carries it throughout your body. If you like cars, think of oxygen as oil that is used to lubricate all of the parts of the machine that is your body. After a warm-up the amount of oxygen in your blood is considerably higher than if you were to just sit around and do nothing. That is very important because during your race, your muscles are going to not only need that extra oxygen; they are going to be screaming for it! Once the oxygen is all used up, your body is forced to find ways to create energy without it, and that is not only inefficient, it's actually painful. The reason you feel soreness in your muscles is because they are unable to use oxygen to create energy. Instead they resort to Anaerobic (without oxygen) respiration. The result is lactic acid. And, if you do not know it by now, lactic acid is *not* your friend. Lactic acid is the chemical that makes muscles hurt, knot up, and causes fatigue.

All of that can be eliminated or greatly reduced simply by taking the time to properly warm up a short time before each event.

TIP: Be sure to do a short warm-up before each of your events and stay active between events to ensure oxygen is evenly distributed to your cells before each swim. Doing so can delay the onset of lactic acid by one full length of your race!

CRAMPS

Another big problem during your race is cramping. How many swimmers out there have had to suffer a major cramp during a race? If you have been fortunate enough to avoid it, you are very lucky. Believe me, it is not something you want. Coach X has seen cases where swimmers have completely stopped in the middle of the pool due to a serious cramping problem. In every case where a swimmer suffers from a cramp during a race, chances are that they did not warm-up properly.

Coach X loves science and it turns out there is a lot of really cool science in cramps. Neat things like sodium-potassium ion pumps, mitochondria and electrolyte imbalances. Things like this make Coach X very excited, but probably don't mean a whole lot to most sprinters. Fortunately there is a pretty easy way to explain why a warm-up helps to prevent cramps. But first, it is important to know what a cramp really is.

CONTRACTION ACTION

In the simplest terms, each of your joints is attached with two muscles. One muscle pulls the joint in one direction, the other pulls in the opposite direction. This allows you to do things like kick your leg up and down. A cramp occurs when the signals to your muscles get confused and causes an over-shortening of a muscle. Cramps can be caused by cold, overexertion or low calcium level in blood (especially for adolescents) though the most common reason is low sodium and potassium levels in blood accompanied by excessive dehydration.

Say what? Okay, let's put it a bit more simply. Do you have a water bottle on deck at all times during practice? Do you keep a banana or some pretzels nearby for a quick snack? While a lot of swimmers do these things they don't really know why they do it. Water is essential to keep your body hydrated and the banana and pretzels provide most of the chemicals your body needs to prevent cramps. If you don't have a water bottle and some snacks high in potassium and calcium you may want to rethink what you bring to practice. But when it comes to races or long practices, *when* you eat and drink plays just a big role in preventing cramps as what you eat as we will see.

TIP: Make sure your sport drink contains REAL sugar! Do not use a zero calorie drink because your brain needs glucose during workout to improve stroke technique. Sugar substitutes do not work in your brain. Without it you will practice bad strokes and swim slower at races.

PLUG IN YOUR MUSCLES

In order for your muscles to work properly, they need to send and receive electric impulses sent from your brain into the muscle fibers. Now you would think that such a thing would be more or less a guarantee. After all, we don't see too many people walking around with random arm and leg spasms. The reason for this is that your body maintains a pretty evenly distributed amount of electrically conductive chemicals in your blood. These are called electrolytes. It's what you get when you drink a sports drink. When the supply of these chemicals is low, the body has trouble signaling the muscles. The result is that the muscles get confused and can end up creating a cramping situation. A warm-up helps to pump blood through your body and delivers the electrolytes more evenly to your muscles to prevent the signals from getting confused. You can think of a warm-up as CPR for your muscles.

PRETZELS AND BANANAS

While we are on the subject, it is probably a good time to mention why so many people recommend eating salty snacks and a banana or two during breaks. These foods contain high amounts of sodium and potassium; both of which are excellent electrolytes that your body needs. Eating these foods and doing a light warm-up to get them into your blood will greatly reduce the risk of cramping during a meet and will very likely give your body an increased ability to distribute energy quickly.

Don't just eat these snacks and sit around. You need to get the electrolytes out of your stomach and into your muscles. That won't happen until you get your body moving. After your snack you need to get into the warm-up pool and get your blood flowing. If there is no warm-up pool then do some light exercise such as jumping jacks, bounces, monkey arm swings or push-ups.

TIP: Did you know that a baked potato has more potassium than a banana!?

TIP: After eating salty snacks or drinking sport drinks, hop in the warm-up pool or do light exercise to distribute the electrolytes. You may be able to swim an extra 25 yards without getting tired if you do!

STRETCHING

In the previous section we learned why doing a warm-up is so important both at meets and at practice. But even with a warm-up, muscles cannot operate at maximum range without first being stretched. Okay, Coach X will admit that this isn't quite true, so let me rephrase this. Muscles cannot be used at maximum range without causing excruciating pain and causing massive muscle damage unless first stretched. Get the point?

PLASTIC MAN

That may be overstating it, but it is true. Muscle fibers need to be stretched before they can operate properly over their full range of motion. To experience this yourself try this:

PLASTIC MAN

Stand up, bend over and attempt to touch your toes. Most people will not make it all the way, and that's fine. Just go as far as you can comfortably. Now hold that spot for 15 seconds.

When you reach 15, without bouncing, give yourself an extra reach. You should now be able to go another inch or two. Hold that for about 10 seconds.

What just happened? How were you just able to get an extra inch or two when you couldn't do that only 15 seconds earlier?

No, you are not plastic man. This simple exercise demonstrates how important it is to warm up. The muscles needed to be stretched before they could properly go through their full range of motion. Coach X is pretty sure you can already figure out why that is important. But, just in case, let me spell it out for you. When you swim it is extremely important that you reach as far as possible on each stroke. Want to out touch your opponent? It goes a lot better when you can actually reach an inch further than the swimmer in the lane next to you. If your muscles are not warmed up and properly stretched, you literally cannot reach as far. A shorter reach means a slower time. It is as simple as that.

TIP: By stretching before your race you will be able to out-touch your opponent by half a second.

PRE-EVENT WARM-UPS

Everyone knows that the general warm-up is important, but don't forget about your pre- race warm up. A few minutes before your event you should take an opportunity to do a race specific warm-up. This will help get your muscles ready for the increased demand that you are about to put on them. Coach X has seen many swimmers that tried to skip this step and it never turns out well. To be a *Super Sprinter* you must do an event specific warm-up and try to finish about seven minutes before your event. Why seven minutes? Okay, Coach X will tell you. And guess what, I'll even do more than that. I will give you a pre-race warm-up that Coach X "guarantees" will drop a full second off of most swimmers' time in the 100! Note that I put guarantee in quotes. That's because I don't really guarantee it, but try it and it should work.

RETRO WARM-UP

They say if you hold on to a thing long enough that it will come back in style. Coach X is hoping that someday his parachute pants will be in style again, but I digress. That is certainly the case with this warm-up. Coach X spends a lot of time doing research. A few years back he came across a study on various pre-event warm-up techniques. The interesting thing was that this particular study was very old. In fact it was from the 1970's. When Coach X read the study he was struck by some of the conclusions that it reached. Not because the study recommended a particular method, but because it did not. Confused? You should be.

It turns out that in the 1970's most swimming strokes were very different than the way *Super Sprinters* swim today. Back then not much attention was given to things such as stroke length, side swimming, balance and rotation. But today all of that has changed. So when Coach X saw a warm-up that had a strange side effect of increasing stroke length while maintaining stroke rate during a race he knew he found something special. The study had concluded that this would not be a good warm-up because it did not meet the intended study goal of increasing stroke rate. Rather the stroke rate stayed pretty much the same. Coach X realized that this warm-up technique was actually perfect for today's *Super Sprinter* for reasons that we will cover later.

Three years ago Coach X started some experiments of his own. He put this new event specific warm-up to the test. The experiment was very simple. He allowed swimmers to choose between their normal pre-event warm-up or Coach X's magic pre-event warm-up. On average those that used Coach X's method dropped a full second more in a 100 yard swim versus those that did not. Wow! This pre-event warm-up soon became known as the magical warm-up.

Now of course not everyone is going to drop a full second in the 100, and of course you can't expect to drop a second each and every time, but for most swimmers you will see a significant improvement in your race time. Remember though, the point is that to be a *Super Sprinter* you need to do some kind of pre-event warm-up: be it the magical warm- up or one that your coach gives to you.

THE SUPER SIMPLE MIRACLE WARM-UP

On late night television Coach X often sees ads for miracle pills that are guaranteed to make you lose weight or build muscle, some even dissolve in water to clean your clothes. Most all of these are bogus and make Coach X very afraid. In general these products don't have a lick of science to support them. If you are like Coach X, you should get very, very skeptical when someone tells you they have a "Super Simple Miracle Warm-Up". But, like I said this one is at least based in science and has been shown to work well in practice. Please remember that a warm-up alone can't make you a *Super Sprinter* but it is one very important tool in your box. My hope is that using this pre-event warm-up will give you a significant improvement and convince you to do full warm-ups all the time.

The warm up is ridiculously simple and that is why I like it so much:
4x 50 SPRINT in the stroke you will race with a 1:00 minute rest interval between each. The timing is what's hard.

The key is to do this set at a very specific time to ensure that the electrolyte balance in your body is optimized for performance and that the muscles are all properly fueled and ready to go.

For any 100 yard event figure out exactly when you will be racing. At a meet, count the number of heats before your next event, look at the times and try to figure out as close as possible your heat's true start time. Then figure out how long it takes you to do a 50 sprint in the stroke you will be racing. Multiply that number by 4 as you will be doing 4x 50 in the warm-up. Still with me? Now add four minutes to the total to account for the rest period between each 50. And finally add 7 minutes rest time before your race start.

Hunh? Are you Serious? What was all that! Okay, let's look at an easy example:

Erin wants to swim the 100 Breast. Her heat will swim at 1:00 PM.
Erin can swim a sprint 50 breast in 35 seconds.

To do 4x 50 would take her 2:20. (:35 x 4 = 2:20)

Add in 4:00 to give her a 1:00 rest interval between each 50 (2:20 + 4:00 = 6:20) Total time for pre-event warm-up is six minutes and twenty seconds.

But she wants to make sure that she finishes the warm-up as close to 7:00 minutes before her event as possible. Adding in the 7:00 gives us a total of: (6:20 + 7:00 = 13:20)

This means that Erin should start her pre-event warm-up 13:20 before her race. She would be okay starting at 12:45 PM to give a little extra time to get into and out of the warm-up pool and get to her event.

By the way, we used this warm-up technique at the Pacific Zone All-Stars, giving the athletes the choice of this warm-up or their standard warm-up. Every athlete using this warm-up technique dropped a minimum of three seconds in their 100 yard swims. Please give it a try, and if it works for you, Coach X also has a scientifically based cure for the hic-cups that he can share with you. – Really!

TANNER'S STORY

It was a typical summer day in Northern California. The pool was a bit small and very crowded. This was Tanner's third meet of the summer and he had already pulled off several new A times. Today he was going for his Junior Olympic time. Aside from having a competitive spirit unlike anyone you've ever met, the one thing most people noticed about this swimmer was his height. Tanner was a lot shorter than many of the kids he typically raced against. Despite this, Tanner swam surprisingly fast and was almost always seeded in the top heats. Many people that did not know Tanner that day probably commented about how short he was compared to all the other swimmers. But it was not Tanner's height that people would remember about him.

Before each event Tanner had a ritual that he would go through. When they called him up to the blocks, Tanner would first begin to pull on the block to perform a long stretch. Then he would start to bang on the block. And I mean he would bang on the block. This kid could turn a starting block into a musical instrument. He would get a beat going and add in a drum roll. At the same time he would start jumping around the block almost as if he were dancing. He would start shaking his arms and his legs at the same time he was carrying out his starting block rhythms. When they blew the whistle to stand on the blocks he waited for all the other swimmers to step up. Then, he, Tanner would jump up on the block swing his arms over his head and clap them together loud enough to be heard across the pool. He would glance to his left and his right while holding his arms over his head and then he would yell at the top of his lungs, "I'M TANNER!"

Believe it or not he did this before every race. And guess what – It Worked! Despite his size, Tanner was almost always in Lane 4 and almost always came in as heat winner. In his pre-race ritual he not only managed to completely psych out kids nearly twice his size, but he also managed to prepare his body perfectly for the race ahead. Coach X isn't saying you need to act exactly like Tanner did, but there are definitely some good ideas in there.

AT THE STARTING BLOCKS

Many swimmers believe that warm-up stops after they leave the warm-up pool. Ah contré.

The warm-up should continue even at the starting block. Coach X really enjoys doing experiments and collecting data; here is another one that you can do at any swimming meet. During a meet, wait for an event in a different age group than your own, walk up and observe the various heats. Look at the swimmers behind the blocks. Pay particular attention to the swimmers that are stretching, hoping around, splashing themselves with water, pounding on the blocks and shaking their limbs. Compare how these swimmers do to versus the others standing next to them. One thing will quickly become very apparent. The swimmers that just stand behind the blocks lose to those that are actively warming up at the starting block.

If you want to be a *Super Sprinter* you need to be one of those people jumping around and splashing themselves with water. Is there a scientific basis for what they are doing? You bet there is! Let's take a look at some of them.

SHAKE IT UP

When you see a swimmer jumping up and down at the starting block or shaking out an arm or a leg, what's really happening? Well, aside from loosening the muscle and stretching those fibers, they are also increasing their heart rate. That in turn drives blood throughout the body which helps to deliver those essential electrolytes we have been talking about. If you remember we made an analogy to a car earlier and discussed how a car needs to have all the parts of the engine well-oiled to run properly. This analogy applies very well here. Imagine that the swimmer jumping and shaking at the block has just turned on his engine. He is revving it up and getting the oil to flow over all the parts. But there is an added benefit here as well. If the swimmer is able to get her pulse to over 120 beats per minute, the oxygen in her system will help with aerobic respiration when she swims. This will delay the onset of lactic acid production by about 25 yards. That means that she will be able to swim one additional length of the pool before her body starts to hurt. Imagine how useful that would be in a 100 butterfly event! So shake that thang!

TIP: Jump around behind the starting block. If you get your pulse to over 120 beats per minute just before your race, you will be able to swim an extra 25 yards before your body starts to hurt!

SPLASH!

You may wonder why some swimmers decide to splash themselves with water before an event. Maybe it is something that you do yourself. Most swimmers that splash themselves with water have absolutely no idea why they do it. Many will tell you that it makes them more slippery when they hit the water. Unfortunately this isn't true. However, it is true that splashing water on your body before your race is often likely to make you go faster! Why?

In case you have not noticed it recently, you are a mammal. Nature didn't really intend for you to do things like jump into a large vat of water and flail around at high speed. Part of being human is that we love to do things that our bodies weren't designed to do. One thing that our bodies *were* designed to do is protect us from our own stupidity. Sometimes these built in body defenses get in the way of what we are trying to accomplish. Since the water we swim in

14

is usually much cooler than the air, our bodies have an immediate response as soon as we dive in. The body is initially shocked and believes that – "oh, oh, silly human you've just put yourself into something really cold. I had better initiate a hypothermic response!" So the body immediately begins to draw blood away from the extremities and into the core organs to protect them from the cold.

This is bad.

It means that all that warming up you just did to get the electrolytes distributed in your body didn't amount to much. Without proper blood flow to your arms and legs the oxygen won't get to where it needs to go either. Your muscles will have to use anaerobic respiration and that means they will produce painful lactic acid very quickly. The end result is that you will get fatigued earlier, sore earlier, and swim much slower.

This is bad.

However, it turns out that we can trick our bodies. Simply by splashing water on yourself prior to the start of the race you trigger this same reaction, but you do it *before* you enter the water. After a few seconds the body realizes that it is not in danger and restores the normal flow of blood. Now when you dive into the cooler water, your body no longer responds with a shock reaction. It knows there is nothing to worry about and all of your oxygen and electrolytes go exactly where they need to be. The result is that you go longer, stronger and faster than you would have without splashing.

That is good.

TIP: If the water is cooler than the air, make sure to splash a LOT of pool water on your body a few seconds before the start of your race.

TIP: If the air feels COLDER than the water – <u>DO NOT SPLASH!</u> If you do, you WILL go slower!

NATALLIE'S STORY

It was a very cold winter day in California where nearly all the pools are outdoor pools. Today the temperature was hovering in the mid-forties! The pool was a fifty meter pool setup for a short course race. They were running two courses simultaneously that day with girls on one side and boys on the other. As is often the case, the boys' side was getting out of synch with the girls side. Normally this would not be a problem. However, just when Natalie's heat was whistled forward several eight and under boys took the whistle to mean "start" and jumped in the water on the other side of the pool. To avoid confusion, the meet referee decided to hold up the events on the girls' side of the pool until the eight and unders were done swimming.

Natalie was shaking because it was so cold. So were all the other girls in her heat. This was one thing that Natalie did not want right now. She was a strong swimmer and was very close to making it onto the all-star team for her zone. This race, she was hoping, was going to put her over the edge against some other girls who were also very close. But now, with this wait, she was starting to wonder. The cold was definitely getting to her.

Seeing this, the meet referee ordered all of the girls to get into the pool to stay warm. As soon as Natalie's coach heard this, he jumped to his feet and yelled across the pool to Natalie, "DO NOT GET IN THE WATER!" The meet referee looked scornfully at the coach. How could he possibly make his swimmer stay out there in the cold? The other girls all jumped in the water and Natalie grabbed her towel and started doing jumping jacks.

After more than five minutes the girls were allowed to exit the pool and continue with the event. Keeping in mind that Natalie never got into the pool in the first place. When the other girls got up on the deck, they were far more cold than before and were all shaking horribly; except Natalie. With the girls now standing behind the blocks, it still took the starter some time to get things ready again. The whole time the other girls' muscles began to tense up; Natalie was relaxed and ready to go. When the call came to "take your mark", Natalie was ready. Not only was she the first one off the block, but her swim was flawless. The other girls, some of whom were seeded much higher than Natalie, were visibly doing very poorly.

At the end of the race, Natalie came in as heat winner by over two seconds! All of the other swimmers in her heat had added time. Once the last swimmer reached the wall Natalie's coach yelled out to the referee, "*and that is why you don't jump in the water when the air is cold!*" Natalie smiled back at her coach. She made the selection for the all-star team over the other girls in her heat.

PRE-RACE TIP SUMMARY

TIP: By stretching before your race you will be able to out-touch your opponent by half a second!

TIP: Be sure to do a short warm-up before each of your events and stay active between events to ensure oxygen is evenly distributed to your cells before each swim. Doing so can delay the onset of lactic acid by one full length of your race!

TIP: Make sure your sport drink contains REAL sugar! Do not use a zero calorie drink because your brain needs glucose during workout to improve stroke technique. Sugar substitutes do not work in your brain. Without it you will practice bad strokes and swim slower at races.

TIP: Did you know that a baked potato has more potassium than a banana!?

TIP: After eating salty snacks or drinking sport drinks, hop in the warm-up pool or do light exercise to distribute the electrolytes. You may be able to swim an extra 25 yards without getting tired if you do!

TIP: Jump around behind the starting block. If you get your pulse to over 120 beats per minute just before your race, you will be able to swim an extra 25 yards before your body starts to hurt!

TIP: If the water is cooler than the air, make sure to splash a LOT of pool water on your body a few seconds before the start of your race.

TIP: If the air feels COLDER than the water – <u>DO NOT SPLASH!</u> If you do, you WILL go slower!

AT THE RACE

STARTS

"Facts which at first seem improbable will, even on scant explanation, drop the cloak which has hidden them and stand forth in naked and simple beauty."

Galileo Galilei

STARTS

Over the years Coach X has worked with athletes from several different sports. I've worked with boxers, runners, and cyclists. I have worked with kids that play soccer, football, baseball, basketball, lacrosse, and even ultimate Frisbee. Each of these athletes came to me wondering if swimming on a team could improve their performance in the other sport. My response is almost always, "YES!" But if you knew Coach X well, you would know that I try to only give a definitive yes or no answer if I have a study to support my statement. While I have studies that show swimming can improve your performance in soccer, football and baseball, I do not yet have any such studies for the other sports. However, as a general rule of thumb the things that swimming does to make you better in football, baseball and soccer generally apply to just about any other sport.

Similarly, I have had many swimmers come to me and ask me what sport is the best sport they can join to help cross train for swimming. Sadly, I have to tell them the answer is: none. Every study that I have ever seen has shown that while swimming has an almost universal improvement on other sports, the converse is not true. This means that participating in any other sport will generally not improve your performance in the pool. The one big exception is where your other sport or training improves your overall body fitness; but more on that later.

While it has been shown that running track or cross country does not greatly improve your performance in swimming, there is one aspect of track that does directly apply to swimming. The most obvious place you will notice this in swimming is during the start.

TIP: The absolute best cross training for swimming is yoga! Yoga for strength training not only increases your core body strength, but also helps you stretch your muscles. Swimmers who practice yoga regularly are faster in all strokes than those that do not.

FLOP RIGHT IN

Back when Coach X was swimming, his coach told him stories of how a perfect "dive" should be performed. This amounted to stepping up on the block, throwing your arms forward and attempting to make as much contact with the surface as possible. Today we call this a belly flop! And, believe it or not, this was actually considered the fastest possible dive not much more than forty years ago! Clearly, things have changed. But wait, get this, there was supposedly actual "science" to support this belly flop method. The hypothesis (notice I did NOT say theory) was that by doing a belly flop, several things occurred that would make the swimmer go faster. First, the initial pain to the system was supposed to shock the muscles and delay the onset of lactic acid (lactic acid is what makes your muscles hurt so badly on the third length of that 100 fly). Secondly, the impact was supposed to get your blood moving away from the heart and out to your extremities. In principle, that at least is a good idea, but today we have better ways of accomplishing this. Finally the belly flop was supposed to be painful causing your brain to release endorphins. These are the chemicals that your brain releases during the so called "second wind". The idea here was that these endorphins would prevent the swimmer from tiring too quickly during the race. So the next time you do a belly flop accidentally into the pool, you can just tell your friends that you were doing an experiment on fast starts! Uhm, by the way, please ***Do Not*** do belly flops and get hurt. Coach X wants you to be a *Super Sprinter* not a super blister!

STEP RIGHT UP

Today there are two main types of starts used by swimmers. One is called the grab start in which the swimmer steps up and places both feet over the front edge of the block, then grabs either between or outside of the feet. The second method is fast becoming the most popular. It is called the track start. In the track start the swimmer steps on the block with only one foot over the leading edge and the other slightly behind – just like a runner in track.

Because we have two starts from which to choose, we can immediately begin to ask a lot of questions. Is one faster than the other? Will one start get you further out into the lane than the other? Will you have a higher chance of false starting with one start or the other?

All of these are very important questions that you as the *Super Sprinter* should be asking. Fortunately, science has provided us with some answers. Before I present you with the results there is one thing of which I need to remind you.

THE FIRST RULE OF THUMB

Remember the first rule of thumb: All thumbs are different. This means that what might apply to 99% of the people in this world, may not apply at all to you. So, after reading this chapter, or anything else in the book, we encourage you to try out the techniques we suggest and decide what works best for *you*.

Coach X firmly believes in applying science first, but once you use the science swimming is just as much an art as dancing or painting. Each of us has so many unique features about us that it is important to remember the science in this book is targeted at swimmers in general. This is to say that if you are an "average", "normal" person, everything you read in this book will apply directly to you and will greatly improve your times. However, there are some Olympic athletes that do things very differently than you will read in this book. In some cases they may well go even faster by changing their stroke. There are some great examples of former Olympians who came back, changed their stroke and won gold for their efforts. But often times an Olympic athlete may have a stroke "flaw" which for them is an advantage.

While Coach X likes to do the analysis and apply science, these athletes depend on being fast for their sponsorships and their income. In some cases it may be that changing to a more scientific method is too scary or will take too long, but in most cases, these athletes swim the way they do because… well, their thumbs are just a little bit different than yours or mine. They do what they do because, for them, it is faster. So we encourage you to try the exercises and experiments in this book, scientifically, everything is guaranteed to work. But it just might be that you're just a little bit different and there just may be a slightly different way of doing things for you that works great. Don't be afraid of being a little different if it works for you, but also don't be afraid of trying something new and scientific to see if it just might make you faster.

TEENAGE MUTANT NINJA SWIMMERS

A long, long time ago we all started out as a small rodent. That rodent changed over time and crawled out from under the ground to up in the trees and eventually became chimps and finally became people. Similarly the Grand Canyon was once just a river running along the ground, but over a lot of time, it became something very beautiful. Remember, swimming is as much art as it is science. Beautiful things take time and effort. In addition, swimming, and therefore how we train, has evolved over time.

With this in mind, Coach X created what he calls, "Mutation Drills". For those who have not participated in one of Coach X's clinics, we do something a little fun on the last day. After taking a week to learn several new techniques, swimmers are encouraged to change just one thing in any drill and see if it has an immediate improvement on their speed. We do this because every once in a while we will find something amazing. Someone in the clinic will do something that actually improves their speed! When we find these mutations, we have the entire group give it a try.

Sometimes we find that the mutation only helps the one swimmer who discovered it. That's great, because it means that swimmer just discovered the rule of thumbs. In this case, Coach X recommends that they keep their mutated stroke drill and use it whenever possible, but only for that one swimmer. However, on rare occasion, the mutation will work for everyone! Coach X loves those moments. When this happens we change the drill for all future clinics. Can you guess what happens next? A whole new set of swimmers gets to perform a mutation set on the new drill and again the entire set of drills continues to evolve over and over to meet the needs of more and more swimmers.

Coach X encourages all of you *Super Sprinters* to do the same thing. After trying the drills, experiments and techniques in this book, when you've truly mastered each item and you are practicing regularly, then maybe once a month try changing something. See what happens. Did it make you faster or slower; why? If it made you faster, have some teammates or friends try your mutation. If it made the group faster, then please write us and share your mutation so that we can share it with the world. We would love to hear your stories at **SBSCSWIM@GMAIL.COM.**

TIP: Use mutation drills to evolve your stroke. After you have mastered a drill, try to change one thing and measure if it makes you faster or slower. Remember a good mutation is a very rare thing.

THE PERFECT START

What makes a start a good start?

Most swimmers already know that the entire purpose of the start is to get out as far as possible into the lane with as much speed as possible. So for our purposes we are going to say that a good start is any start that accomplishes that goal.

SUPER SOAKERS AND GARDEN HOSES

When Coach X was a young boy, his mother often yelled at him for playing in the water. He would often volunteer to wash the dishes in the sink just so that he could have fun splashing around with the sprayer connected to the sink.

Outside he would turn on the hose and shoot water up as high as he could into the air, then try to run away before the water would fall on his head. Playing with water is fun. One day while playing with the hose outside, Coach X decided to see how far he could spray the water.

You see, Coach X has a younger brother and that brother was sleeping in a nearby lawn chair. This became too good a target to pass up. The first thing Coach X tried was shooting the water up into the air, hoping that the wind would blow it toward his little brother. It didn't. Next he thought he would just shoot the water straight at his sleeping brother. The water stream went a lot closer, but was just short of hitting his prey. Finally he decided to try a combination. Young Coach X pointed the hose about half way between up and straight at his brother to make a forty-five degree angle, then pulled the trigger on the spray gun and..... SPLAT! Got him!

I NEVER STUDIED THE LAW

The question is, why didn't the water hit when it was aimed directly at the lawn chair? This is an important question because every new swimmer goes through a similar experience. The first time a young swimmer steps onto the block they look down at the water and think, "Ok, I need to get in that water and jump out as far as I can." And in principal, that is true. Now, maybe it is from watching too many Saturday morning cartoons, but most swimmers forget about the law of gravity. It's just like when a cartoon character walks over a cliff and continues to walk off in midair and says "I never studied the law!" Well, it happens that Coach X did study law, but that's another story.

In case you've forgotten, we live in the real world. We aren't cartons, and guess what? We need to remember gravity. It's that force that is keeping your bottom firmly planted to that chair or sofa that you are on right now. Without it, we could weightlessly hover or float around, and well, the water wouldn't like staying in the pool very much. It is because of gravity that we cannot simply jump straight off of a starting block and expect to have a good dive. It is also because of gravity that the water Coach X shot straight at his little brother did not reach him. Gravity pulled down on the water and made it hit the ground before it reached the lawn chair. Similarly, when you jump straight off the block, gravity will pull you down before you get too far out into the lane.

So what is the solution? Many of you already know. You need to get as much height as possible along with as much distance as possible. The result is a parabolic entry. Think of it as making an arch as you fly through the air. Pretty simple stuff right? And of course the best way to do that is to jump out at a forty-five degree angle, right? Well, actually while that's almost correct, you would in fact be wrong.

People will argue that due to the weight distributions, center of gravity, kinetic force of legs, and so on, that the optimal angle of release for a swimmer to achieve maximum distance off the block is NOT forty-five degrees. In reality there is a much simpler reason. You are not starting at the same level as the surface of the water! Because of this, the optimal angle to jump off the block is really about forty-three degrees. Remember that the surface of the pool is *never* at the same height as the starting block. That means a regular parabola won't get you the optimal distance. Instead, you need to compensate for the fact that the starting point (the block) is higher than the ending point (the water). To optimize your distance in this situation you will need to take off at an angle slightly lower to the water (or around 43 degrees from the pool deck). I will wait while you get out your measuring devices.

TIP: The best angle of launch from a starting block is about forty degrees. Launching slightly lower than forty-five degrees will get you out further than your competition!

Okay – maybe that's a bit silly, but it's still good to know that science has our back even when it comes to something as seemingly simple as starts. But consider this: As a *Super Sprinter* you know that every millisecond in swimming counts. Races are won and lost by the hundredth of a second, and believe me, those two degrees will make at least one hundredth of a second difference! At least knowing this, you may be able to position your body differently and pick up a win.

TIP: Never just dive down toward the water! Don't dive straight out. Always dive up in an arch!

DISTANCE PER START

Now that we know the best angle of launch we can start to answer one of the questions about track starts versus grab starts. Will one of these starts get you to that magic forty- three degree take off angle easier than the other? The answer is yes.

After measuring the launch angles of several swimmers using a video camera, you will find that more often than not, the grab start generally gets swimmers closer to the best angle of launch. For new swimmers learning to dive, this is almost universally true. Video analysis of the track start shows that it generally results in a much lower angle of launch meaning that the swimmer will not get as far out into the lane. So on the question of which start will get you further into the lane faster, the hands down winner is the grab start. However, for some swimmers who have grown up practicing the track start, they may have learned to overcome the launch angle and may be able to achieve the same distance and speed off the block as a grab start.

But wait, it gets even more complicated. At least one study shows that the vertical (up and down) speed at which you leave the block is slightly faster with a track start than with a grab start. Another study showed that swimmers with a track start generally had a higher speed at the five meter mark than those with a grab start. The problem was that those studies didn't say where the swimmers were entering the water.

As we know, as soon as you hit, you begin to slow down. So if the grab start gets you out further than a track start, it may well be that the track start swimmers had already begun kicking. If that's the case, had the study measured just a bit further they would have found the grab start swimmer was faster. Yes, science can get very confusing when there are conflicting studies. Don't worry; Coach X will look at a few other factors before we reach a conclusion on which start is better than the other.

TIP: Grab starts generally result in greater distance from the starting block.

DISTANCE PER START

How can you tell if a grab start or a track start is right for you? It's pretty simple really. Setup a video camera and film yourself doing several of each dive. Make sure that your camera is stationary. Mount it to a fixed location (like the bleachers or a table), or setup a tri-pod. Have your coach or a friend use a whistle or loud beep to indicate when you should go.

After doing about ten of each type of dive, review the tape. I recommend playing back the video on a larger television rather than using the camera viewfinder. The first thing to examine is where you entered the water. Do you notice a difference between the two types of dives?

Finally use a protractor (that is a plastic device used to measure angles), and actually measure the angle at which you leave the starting block. Do you notice one dive giving you a launch angle closer to 43°? If so, you should probably stick with that dive. If you want to try a really cool program to measure your angle, try visiting http://strokelab.finisinc.com/

REACTION TIME

The next question we will ask is about reaction time. How quickly can you get off the block? Which of the two starts will get you up in the air and into the water faster? Again, the use of video equipment makes this very easy to test.

Using the same video footage you made above, time how long it takes for both of your feet to leave the starting block after the whistle or beep. If you are like most swimmers you will find that the track start is noticeably slower than a proper grab start. Why? Because, when you execute a track start you do not distribute the weight of your body equally on both feet at once. Rather, you shift the weight from one foot to the other, resulting in a delay of the back foot releasing from the block. In the grab start, you should be resting your entire body weight on the balls of your feet. The slightest meow from the neighbor's cat should be enough to send you on your way. Because both feet take the body weight equally and the release force is equally distributed between both feet, you will leave the block slightly faster in a grab start.

Again, Coach X wants to point out that there are studies that show that college women using the track start were able to get off the blocks faster, but the study didn't say whether this was the standard start for these girls, and Coach X is willing to bet that it was. As mentioned earlier, a grab start is almost always faster, but you can learn to get off the block just as fast with a track start. Furthermore, if you haven't practiced a grab start in a while, you may very well be slower if you forgot how to properly balance on the balls of the feet. If you're just starting out, Coach X recommends working with the grab start. Video footage from many, many swimmers (several more than used in the college study) has shown Coach X that the grab start has a faster reaction time for most swimmers. Getting off the block fast after the starter has sounded is clearly very important to your overall time. Therefore, in general, doing a grab start will get you a slightly better time.

TIP: Grab starts generally have a faster reaction time off the block.

STABILITY

Our last question was whether or not one start is inherently more stable than the other? Or, put differently, will one start increase your chances of getting disqualified due to a false start. The answer again is, yes. With the grab start getting you a better distance per start and a better reaction time, you may wonder why so many people teach the track start at all. The answer is simple: It is more stable.

The track start balances the body in a more stable manner on the starting block, allowing you to shift your weight between your front and rear foot. You feel very firmly planted on the starting block when doing a track start and the chances of you losing your balance and falling in are nearly zero.

On the other hand, the grab start requires that you really take time to find the perfect balance point on your feet. You need to be just at the edge of falling in the water without actually doing so. The slightest false sound could send you hurtling into the water and the slightest maladjustment could find you in the water before the starter sounds. Grab starts are tricky to learn and take time to do well. Once you master it, the grab start is often a better choice.

Because track starts are more stable, easier to teach and result in fewer DQs, they are taught more often than grab starts. In addition, with a lot of practice a swimmer can make a track start just as good as a grab start. If you have time and patience or if you are a new swimmer learning to dive, we recommend you take the time to learn the grab start. Try them both, find what works for you and in then stick with it.

One more point about the track start. While it is true that the start is more stable and therefore you are less likely to false start due to falling in the water, there is a problem. New swimmers often tend to rock back in forth while doing a track start. Once the starter says, "take your mark," swimmers are required to remain completely still. In the past many referees would ignore younger swimmers moving on the block. Not so anymore! In many states and in many zones *any* rocking action at all during a track start will get you disqualified. So if you are going to use the track start, practice striking a pose and freezing like a statue until you hear the starting beep!

TIP: When doing a track start, do not rock back and forth or shift weight between feet. Once the starter says, "take you mark," you need to become absolutely still or risk disqualification!

LEARNING TO FLY

Are there any good ways to learn to dive better? I'm quite certain that if you were to ask this question to five different coaches, you would get five different answers. Every coach and every team has a different process for teaching starts. The following is not from a scientific study, but comes from my own experiences in working with thousands of swimmers over the years. You may already have found a much better way to teach starts, and if you have, please pass on your knowledge so that we can tell others. If you haven't yet found a great method of learning your starts, then I hope this section helps you to become a *Super Sprinter* start master!

VISUALIZE

Before you even try diving into the water close your eyes and imagine what it is going to look like. Imagine yourself stepping up to the blocks, reach up and clap your hands over your head to verify that you are longer than your opponents. Do a little shake down to loosen up your body. Take a look over the flag line. Now look out ahead into the lane and pick your entry point. Imagine yourself launching in a perfect arch going up into the air, above the flags and then curving down to enter the water right on your point. Got that? Okay – then let's do it.

BODY POSITION

I am going to describe a grab start here. You want to step up onto the block and stand with your feet just wider than your shoulders. Stand as close to centered (left to right) as you can. Walk to the front edge of the block and place your toes over the front edge of the block. Now just do a quick check and make sure your feet are not too close together or too far apart – remember shoulder width is a good starting point.

When you hear the starter say "Take your mark!" you will reach down and "grab" the starting block with your hands between your feet or outside your feet. Generally you will want to do the grab start by grabbing between your feet. Try both ways to find what feels best to you. Older swimmers may not be able to grab outside the feet. The taller and wider you are, the more space you are going to take on the block and there may be no space left for your hands to be placed outside your feet.

Many swimmers will "grab" the starting block with their fingers and place their thumbs on the block. I do not recommend this. When I tell my swimmers to "grab" the block, I want them to simply place their hand in front and touch the block. No grabbing, and in fact I insist that the thumbs must be in front too. Why? Because I do not want anything to create extra drag or delay in getting off that block. If you grab on the block, you must first release your grip before you can launch. If your hands are in front and not grabbing, you can still use them to push or throw, without having to release them. This saves you a hundredth of a second or so. And as we all know, hundredths of a second matter a lot in swimming!

TIP: When doing a start, do NOT grab the block! The act of releasing your grip takes extra time. While it may not feel like it; you will go much faster throwing your arms up and forward versus rocking, grabbing and pulling.

Now you need to balance your body. Tuck your head down low and look between your legs at what is behind you. Push your hips up as high as you possibly can. Bend your elbows and relax. This will set you up in a slightly unbalanced position. You will need to find the right place on your feet to hold your balance. Begin to lean forward until you feel that you are just about to fall in, and then hold it. You should be at the point where if the swimmer behind you sneezed she would blow you into the pool. Finding this spot without falling in takes time. So when you are learning, have a friend or coach help to lean your body forward. When you begin to fall into the pool have them lean you back to the point at which you can hold your body up without falling. As you practice you will become able to lean further and further.

Staying loose and relaxed is very important. Do not stiffen your body. This is one of the reasons for bending the elbows. It helps to remind you that you need to be loose. It also helps to get you into a more compact and spring like body position.

Now you can wait for the starter. When you hear the horn, you should pretend that you are *not* on the starting block, but rather that you are on a trampoline. Pretend that there is an invisible starting block at the level of your head and just in front of you. You will jump off the trampoline, onto the invisible, hovering starting block, and *then* you will dive into the pool. Doing this will prevent you from making the number one mistake in diving. You should *not* try to dive directly into the pool from the starting block. Instead, you should jump upward and outward. The trampoline, invisible block approach works very well when you combine it with a quick glance above the flag line.

When you finally hear the starter horn, throw your hands forward and up into the air. As you begin to fall forward, fully and quickly extend your legs to full length. In other words – jump! As you begin to jump look up over the flag line and try to direct your body up rather than into the pool. Next, quickly get your head under your arms. You want to do this before or at the highest point in your arch.

Once you reach the highest point of your arch, angle down into the pool for a shallow angle

28

entry. Bend your body slightly (like a boomerang) to get your head under your feet. Then straighten your body for a nice entry. You do not want to enter the pool straight up and down. You don't want to enter completely flat either! You need to have a slight angle to your entry so that you can enter and stay shallow.

Mark the point at which you entered the water and try it again. Keep practicing until you can get all the way out to the flag line with just the dive. Then add a streamline to your dive and see how much further out you can get. Your first goal should be getting to the end of the first fifteen meter mark on your dive when combined with a streamline. And don't forget to streamline your feet!

TIP: With practice, most swimmers can develop the advantages of the grab start in a track start or vice versa.

STARTS SUMMARY

TIP: The best angle of launch from a starting block is about forty degrees. Launching slightly lower than forty-five degrees will get you out further than your competition!

TIP: Never just dive down toward the water! Don't dive straight out. Always dive up in an arch!

TIP: Grab starts generally result in greater distance from the starting block.

TIP: Grab starts generally have a faster reaction time off the block.

TIP: When doing a track start, do not rock back and forth or shift weight between feet. Once the starter says, "take you mark," you need to become absolutely still or risk disqualification!

TIP: With practice, most swimmers can develop the advantages of the grab start in a track start or vice versa.

STREAMLINES

"Intelligence is the ability to adapt to change."
Stephen Hawking

STREAMLINES

Streamlines!? You have got to be kidding me. I already know how to do a streamline; I've been doing them from day one, so I'm going to skip this chapter. Fair enough, you should feel free to skip this chapter. After all, Coach X is certain that you are not one of the 99.9% of all swimmers that do streamlines incorrectly. Certainly you don't just place your arms over your head, overlap your hands and tuck your head. Because of course, if that's what you do, then you would *NOT* be doing a streamline. What's that? That *is* what you do? Well, then you had better keep reading!

ROCKETSHIPS AND KRYTPONITE

Most swimmers learn to streamline very early in their swimming career. Just go into nearly any learn to swim program and you will hear the instructors telling the young kids to jump up like a rocket with their hands over their heads in the shape of a nose cone. While this is true, you would hardly know it from going to most swimming practices. Most swimmers look like Superman when they push off of the wall – looking straight ahead with one or both arms straight out in front.

In fact, the one thing that Coach X hears more than anything else when traveling around the country and even around the world is coaches yelling "Streamline!" It seems to be the one thing that we as swimmers can just never remember to do. Whether it is off of a start, or off of a turn, many swimmers just don't do it, or don't do it well.

The funny thing is just about every swimmer I have met knows how to do a pretty good streamline. In practice however, many swimmers just get lazy. So starting today, if you are going to truly be a *Super Sprinter* you will need to make a pledge to yourself. Repeat the following until you actually believe it:

"I will do streamlines on EVERY start and at EVERY wall."

You have so many opportunities each day to practice streamlining that there really is no excuse for not making this the very first thing you do to become a *Super Sprinter*. It's easy to do and makes an absolutely huge difference in your overall time. Remember, practice never makes perfect, it makes habit; one very good habit to have is streamlining off of every wall.

Without making the commitment to practice your streamline you will not only look like Superman while pushing off from the wall, but the streamline will become your own personal Kryptonite (The one and only thing that could cripple the man of steel). Poor streamlining can be a very serious problem. For example, you may have an absolutely fantastic turn only to ruin it all by coming to a nearly full stop in the water due to a poor streamline. The same is true for an excellent start where you enter the water further out than anyone else, only to be passed because your attempt at a streamline slows you down so much. Don't let this happen! Commit to doing streamlines off of every wall.

TIP: Make it a point that on your first breath off every wall you do a self-check; ask, "Did I streamline correctly?" If not, go back and do it again. Never leave a wall without having done a proper streamline. If you connect your self-check to your first breath, you will never forget again!

GLIDERS, JACKS, PYRAMIDS AND ARROWS

Coach X is not really surprised by what he sees when he asks almost any swimmer to demonstrate a good streamline. Very few swimmers ever get it correct. But it turns out that even very few experienced swimmers get it correct. In fact Coach X estimates that only about 1 in every 300 swimmers gets it right. Let's see if you are one of those that know. When I say, "Show me a streamline," what do you do?

If you stand up and put your arms straight up over your head like superman, you failed. If however you put your hands over your head like the cone of a rocket, squeeze your elbows tightly, stretch as far as you can, and get your whole head under your arms, then give yourself a pat on the back. You have successfully demonstrated what ½ of a streamline looks like. What? That's right – if you are a swimmer that is only focusing on the arms, you have also failed. This is where about 299 out of 300 swimmers go wrong. It's not a bad form mind you, just not the fastest.

So that brings up the question… what *IS* the fastest form?

Well of course Coach X will tell you, but not without first doing some experiments. Coach X just loves experiments. It's really the only way to prove to yourself that something works. Coach X encourages you to test anything that you are told or read for yourself.

Remember that everyone is somewhat unique so what might work well for some people may not work well for you. In this case however, we are dealing with the laws of physics, so if these experiments don't work for you, really, you should contact NASA or the Nobel committee – they'll definitely want to speak with you!

STREAMLINES

PYRAMIDS

Let's start with something that we could all probably agree just isn't a very good idea. Go ahead and keep your arms in the shape of a rocket cone, squeezed tightly together. When you push off from the wall, make sure you are looking down. Start with your legs spread apart as far as possible – and as far as comfortable if you are a boy! Push off from the wall like this and measure how far you travel from the wall. Coach X refers to this as the pyramid "streamline".

JACKS

Now let's do another simple experiment. For some reason swimmers seem to like this test the best. Here is how it goes: Using the same legs as above, spread your arms as far apart as possible. Note: You don't have to make them into a 'T', you can make a 'V' if you prefer. Do whatever is more comfortable for you. Once you've got yourself in position, push off and again mark your position at the place you stop. Coach X won't tell you if this will be further or shorter than the last test; he will leave it for you to find out.

GLIDERS

For our third test we will push off from the wall with our legs together. In fact, please be certain to overlap your feet just as you may be used to overlapping your hands. On this test however you are going to place your arms as far apart as possible. This time, Coach X recommends the 'T' configuration, but again if this is hard for you, go ahead and try it with a 'V' configuration. As before, mark how far you were able to get from the wall. Are you surprised by this result?

ROCKETS

For our final test, we are going to do a "traditional" streamline. That is to say that you are going to make a rocket cone with your arms and push off from the wall as you would normally do for a streamline. Mark your position from the wall.

Now that we have some data from our tests, let's go over the results. First of all, Coach X suspects that some swimmers out there are going to be very surprised. Many swimmers are shocked to find that they actually go pretty far doing gliders, at least further than you might expect. The Jacks are usually a total disaster and that really shouldn't be much of a surprise. Pyramids are not that great either. In fact, if you did everything correct, they should have turned out measurably worse than doing a glider. This is the one result that most swimmers don't quite understand. The best of our tests should have been the Rocket.

But is this the best streamline? Actually – No. It isn't. This is the streamline that most swimmers use right now. But since you want to become a *Super Sprinter*, Coach X will now tell you a couple of secrets about streamlines to help you get even more out of them. But before you read on, it is important that you try the experiments or what we are going to say probably won't make much sense to you.

HAPPY FEET

From our experiments we found that spreading our arms out did not slow us down nearly as much as spreading our legs out. This poses a big question; Why? Most people would think it would be exactly the opposite: With your arms out you are slowing yourself down almost immediately, whereas with your legs out you are cutting through the water and it can just flow around the legs like a wake. But that's where those wonderful laws of physics and fluid dynamics come in. To make it very simple – over simple really – it comes down to this… what happens in the first ¼ of your body doesn't really matter as much as what happens in the last ¾. This is very surprising, but it is true. Now Coach X is not saying that a Superman is better than a rocket cone, but it is true that a glider is better than a pyramid. Now that you know this, you may already have figured out that there is a faster way to do a streamline than what most people are doing.

By these simple laws of physics, it soon becomes clear that you can get out noticeably further and faster by not only streamlining your arms, but also by streamlining your legs and your feet. Just as you are taught to overlap and interlock your hands on a streamline, so should you overlap your feet. Just as you are taught to squeeze your arms, so too should you squeeze your legs. Go ahead and try it right now and I bet you will see a small, but noticeable improvement in both distance and time!

TIP: Overlap your feet and squeeze your legs during a streamline to get extra distance off the start and every turn!

HIPS

As mentioned above squeezing is important. Many swimmers remember to squeeze their legs, but never squeeze their buttocks. You will see noticeable improvement in both speed and distance if, when you push off, you focus on squeezing your buttocks (rear end) as tightly as possible. Now far be it for Coach X to say that anyone has a big butt; however, muscle fluctuation does add drag. By squeezing you will eliminate that fluctuation, cut down drag, and go faster.

TIP: Squeeze your hips (butt) on all streamlines! Muscle fluctuation adds drag.

DEPTH

There is an optimal depth at which to streamline. You want to get deep enough that you are not affected by the wake turbulence at the top of the water. However, you also want to be shallow enough that you are not going to have to force yourself to the surface to get air. One of the biggest mistakes that Coach X regularly sees is a swimmer that does not "naturally" surface, but rather uses arms or legs to force themselves to the surface.

A good rule of thumb is to use the target on the wall (The plus sign on the wall on each end of the lane) as a depth gage. Because this target must be placed at the same depth in all pools, you can use it to judge how deeply to place your feet when doing a turn and when doing a streamlined push-off. When doing your push-offs and breakouts, try to place your feet just under the horizontal (long flat) part of the plus mark on the wall. This position is deep enough to avoid wave turbulence and wake forces from the surface, and shallow enough to allow your body to rise naturally to the surface without the need to force yourself to the surface.

WHICH SIDE ARE YOU ON?

The next question that Coach X will answer is the age old question of which is faster: streamlining on your stomach, side or back? If you skipped ahead in the book, shame on you! But you will already know the answer. For those that are following along in the intended order get ready for some more experiments. Remember, anytime a coach or another swimmer tells you something will work for you; always test it to make sure. That is why Coach X puts all these wonderful experiments in here just for you.

ROTAION AND STREAMLINES

What are you waiting for? Let's get started. For the next set of experiments you will need to push-off from the wall first doing your best streamline on your stomach. If you have access to some video equipment, it is always best to film where you end up.

Repeat the experiment by doing the same streamline, but this time on your side. Finally, you will want to do the experiment on your back. If you are not using a video camera, be certain to mark your final position after each streamline.

Unless you are an alien from another world that has figured out how to defy the laws of physics, then the best streamline should have come when you were on your side. But why?

TIP: Always streamline and body dolphin on your side when possible! You will go noticeably further on every start and turn. Getting out further than your opponent off every start and turn wins races!

DEPTH CHARGES

As you may remember, when Coach X was younger, he loved to play in the water and try to get his younger brother wet. One year Coach X and his brother were at a lake playing with a beach ball. It didn't take Coach X too long to realize that if he pushed the beach ball down into the water it would pop out; way out of the water. Properly aimed and timed, the ball could pop out and land right on Coach X's little brother! Perfect!

Eventually Coach X's little brother decided to try the same thing. From watching Coach X push the ball down just a little bit in the water he observed how it would pop, so Coach X's little brother decided to grab the ball, swim to the bottom of the lake and release the ball once Coach X was directly above. Coach X's brother thought that by taking the ball lower, it would shoot up even faster and really smash into Coach X. Aren't you glad you don't have a little brother like that?

What happened surprised both Coach X and his brother. When the ball was released at the bottom of the lake it did not come rushing to the surface. Instead it was much, much, much slower to come to the surface. Once it came to the top, the ball didn't even pop out of the water. It barely broke the surface. This was completely opposite of what Coach X's little brother thought would happen. But what he failed to realize is that by taking the ball all that way down to the bottom, it had to pass through all of the water that was on top of it. Even though the ball was full of air, it was like trying to take a flat kick board and push it up from the bottom of a pool. There was just way too much water resistance. In other words: massive drag!

DEPTH CHARGES

If you want to try this yourself, go ahead and grab a beach ball or kickboard and take it to your next practice. First try pushing it down just a little bit so that it is not completely under water, then let go. Watch how high the ball goes. Next swim the ball to the bottom of the deepest part of the pool and let it go. Measure how high it goes now. There's quite a difference.

If you were a good observer you would have noticed something else as well. When the ball is coming up from a depth, its path to the surface becomes very irregular and uncontrolled. There are reasons for this, but they are a bit complicated. To see an even better example of this bizarre ascent, try the same experiment with a kickboard. Just make sure no one else is around in the pool when you do it!

TIP: Always streamline at a depth that is just below the horizontal cross line of the wall target. This will avoid surface turbulence while still making surfacing level an easy task.

THE ONE DOLLAR CHALLENGE

What does all of this mean for our streamline? Well imagine that your body is like that beach ball or kickboard. If you push off underwater, you are going to want to surface at some point. If you are flat such as when you are on your stomach or back, then you are creating more surface area that has to push up through the water. This creates a lot of drag and slows you down considerably. Therefore, the best streamline you can do is actually on your side. Not your stomach and not on your back.

Now Coach X knows what you are probably thinking. You are saying, "Okay, then to solve this all I need to do is not push off so deeply". Some of you might be thinking, "All I need to do is surface sooner." Both of those ideas seem to make sense, but both would be very bad ideas. Remember, that a swimmer is much faster under water than above it.

But wait! You have all been to meets where you have seen a swimmer that stays underwater a long time and finally surfaces only to come up a full body length behind everyone else. Yep; you better believe that happens all the time. It is important to remember that you want to break the surface just *before* you start to slow down. But, the next time you see it happen in a meet where someone stays underwater for a long time either on a start or on a turn, watch carefully to see if they are streamlining on their side or on their stomach before they break.

If they are behind by a body length or more, Coach X will be $1.00 that they were not on their side. If they are under for a long time and then break ahead of the pack, Coach X will be that same $1.00 that they were streamlining on their side! And for those of you planning to deliberately go out and streamline slowly on your side just to collect you $1.00, forget about it! Coach X doesn't gamble.

HOW LONG IS TOO LONG?

The next question that the *Super Sprinter* should now be asking is "How long should I streamline?" The answer is simple. You should streamline underwater for as long as it is legal to do so and remain fast. Depending on your swimming league and stroke, the rules will vary. As a rule of thumb, Coach X says that you should be able to streamline to the 15 meter mark at the far end of the pool (or at least two thirds of a length). That way you can always do less, and you are guaranteed that you can make the longest distance permitted by the rules.

YOU'RE FULL OF HOT AIR

Now, if you say that there is no way you could ever streamline that far, then Coach X has a neat little trick that you should try. Most swimmers will automatically take a really super deep breath when they are trying to streamline further. That's not a good idea because the increased air turns your lungs into a giant balloon. This changes your buoyancy and makes it so that your body wants to surface very quickly. If you are pulled to the surface by buoyancy you will not be able to streamline very far.

38

Instead, a better strategy is to nearly empty your lungs of air when you push off on a streamline. This will help to keep your body neutrally buoyant, allowing you to stay underwater for a much longer time. You will surface only when you want to surface. Because you can stay under longer, you can get out much further. Coach X is not saying this is necessarily an easy thing to do well, but it is an easy thing to do in general.

To get the most from this technique requires practice. You will need to develop the ability to go with little oxygen for about two thirds of the pool length. But after only a few weeks of practice, most swimmers are able to do this without much problem. Next you will want to learn to do that distance while powering your underwater kick the entire time. This requires a lot of anaerobic or hypoxic (without oxygen) training.

Ask your coaches, and I am sure they will be very happy to accommodate your practice schedule with some anaerobic sets to help you out. Once you have done all of that, then go ahead and take a regular (not deep) breath and let the air out as you streamline. This will allow you to get out even further, although you may need a slightly deeper initial push-off. Before long you'll be going two-thirds of a length without going hypoxic.

After a short while these streamlining techniques will get you out further than anyone else in the pool and you will get their faster! Mastering the streamline is a fantastic way to drop a lot of time in races and is essential to you becoming a *Super Sprinter!*

TIP: Do not streamline with your lungs full of air! Exhale most of your air before you push off from the wall or exhale quickly as you push off to stay under water longer in your streamline.

STREAMLINE TIP SUMMARY

TIP: Make it a point that on your first breath off every wall you do a self-check; ask, "Did I streamline correctly?" If not, go back and do it again. Never leave a wall without having done a proper streamline. If you connect your self-check to your first breath, you will never forget again!

TIP: Overlap your feet and squeeze your legs during a streamline to get extra distance off the start and every turn!

TIP: Squeeze your hips (butt) on all streamlines! Muscle fluctuation adds drag.

TIP: Always streamline and body dolphin on your side when possible! You will go noticeably further on every start and turn. Getting out further than your opponent off every start and turn wins races!

TIP: Always streamline at a depth that is just below the horizontal cross line of the wall target. This will avoid surface turbulence while still making surfacing level an easy task.

TIP: Do not streamline with your lungs full of air! Exhale most of your air before you push off from the wall or exhale quickly as you push off to stay under water longer in your streamline.

TURNS

"Sit down before fact as a little child, be prepared to give up every conceived notion, follow humbly wherever and whatever abysses nature leads, or you will learn nothing."

Thomas Huxley

TURNS

Coach X recalls an event back in the late 1980's. It was during a state high school sectionals meet in the Midwest. The fastest high school swimmers gathered for their shot at a spot on their school's state team. The pool was a very nice pool for the area and was designed without gutters so that the waves would roll right up onto drains on the deck. The swimmers were told that this meant it was a "fast" pool because it eliminated wave reflection. Coach X, as visiting alumni, was allowed down on the deck to view the action up close. Coach X's Alma matter (his old high school) had developed a backstroke swimmer that was one of the fastest in the state at that time and he was expected to break a personal best at this meet. We will call him Tim.

TIM'S STORY

At the start of the race the swimmer stood up on the deck and grabbed the starting block bars. Yes, you were allowed to do a standing backstroke start back then. When the cap gun went off the swimmer did a fantastic entry into the water and was off. When all the swimmers surfaced it was clear that Tim was a full body length ahead of everyone. He got his arms moving very fast and there was a cloud of white water being churned up in his wake. He approached the first wall, reached out, spun on the surface and pushed off on the surface.

He was still in the lead. During the second length another swimmer began to pass just as they came to the wall. But Tim's turn was too fast. After the push off Tim again lead by a full body length. This battle continued through the third length where once again Tim battled his opponent to the wall; then came the last turn. BAM! Tim was off the wall, but this time he didn't get out nearly as far as on his previous turns. About half way into the fourth length the boy in lane five caught up with Tim. Out of the corner of his eye Tim saw this and reached down deep inside for an extra burst of speed for the finish. His whole body was aching and screaming for him to stop. But he did not stop.

Tim sped into the finish. BAM! He touched the wall and beat his personal best time! He had won the race and was definitely going to the state meet. But Tim didn't get out of the pool. He was crying. It took the spectators a few moments to realize that he wasn't crying in tears of joy, but rather tears of pain. The area around the wall where Tim stood was filling with red. It was blood. On the third turn, Tim got too close to the wall. His knuckles hit slightly past the wall and landed on the deck at full force.

Not only had Tim missed his turn, he had broken the knuckles in his right hand and tore them open, in addition he had a good gash in his head. Despite this he had continued to swim and still managed to win his race.

Unfortunately Tim did not go to the state meet. After breaking his knuckles he was unable to swim again for the rest of the season.

Tim's story actually was not unique. It was incidents like this one that eventually lead to the rule change that now permits backstroke swimmers to turn onto their stomachs for their turns.

We can expect that over time there will continue to be rule changes in starts, turns and finishes to help protect our athletes. The information Coach X is about to give on turns is both specific enough and general enough that it should help you become a *Super Sprinter* even if the rules change again in the future. But please, learn from Tim and never compromise on safety when doing a start, turn or finish.

CHANGING TURNS

A word about turns. They have definitely changed over the years. When Coach X swam in high school it was not legal to turn onto your stomach in backstroke when doing a turn. Only a few years ago it was not legal to do a body dolphin during breast stroke and now FINA is deciding whether it is okay to allow up to three body dolphins off the wall in breast.

Over the years we have devised all sorts of interesting ways to reverse direction in a hurry. Thirty years ago, many swimmers chose to do a back flip, much like the front crawl's forward flip. The other backstroke turn at that time, and the one that Coach X preferred, was a rotational surface spin turn. You simply swam up to the wall going full speed, touched with your hand and spun in place on the surface of the water, then pushed off with everything you've got and away you went. This was Coach X's secret weapon because he was double jointed! Coach X was able to go into a turn at full speed and bend his fingers all the way backward against the wall then use them like a spring during the push-off, getting him significantly further out than anyone else – another example of the rule of thumbs (or in this case fingers)!

As you might imagine, there was a big problem with this type of turn. Because it made the swimmer get all the way to the wall and touch with the hand, there were many swimmers with swollen and broken knuckles, not to mention broken fingers and concussions. Today, the backstroke swimmer is allowed to turn over onto the stomach when doing the turn.

Turns don't seem all that difficult to many swimmers, yet to some they are the worst part of a race. It may seem pretty simple when you think about it. Just get to the wall, touch and turn the other direction. But if that was all there was to it, each of us would be a *Super Sprinter* already. In truth, there is a lot to a turn. It doesn't matter if it is a front flip, back flip, spin turn, or open turn. Each has some subtleties that will make the turn faster or slower.

As a rule of thumb, Coach X tries to get his swimmers to complete a turn in less than 1.0 second. That is for *any* turn, including an open turn, back turn or flip turn. Test yourself and see how well you do. Have a friend or a coach use a stop watch. You start at the middle of the pool and as soon as you begin, your helper should start the stopwatch. The moment you start the turn, have your helper hit the split button on the watch. The moment both of your feet clear the wall, have the helper hit the split button a second time.

Most watches will display the split interval. This difference in splits is your turn time. To help with accuracy the helper must start the first split at the same point each time. In backstroke, this should be the moment the swimmer rolls onto the stomach. For breast and fly it is the moment the hands touch the wall. In Front Crawl the turn starts the moment the swimmer begins to tuck the head for the roll. In any stroke, if the total turn takes more than a second, you need to practice it until you can bring it down. At first you are probably going to think it just isn't possible, but after only a few hours of practicing, you will almost certainly get at least one turn under a second.

Most of the swimmers that Coach X has worked with generally start out around 1.6 seconds per turn. Some younger swimmers are even over 2.0 seconds per turn. But after a little practice, almost everyone is able to pull off a .80 or better on every turn. Coach X calls this the "Sub Zero Club".

Imagine if you could take off 2.4 seconds on a 100 yard swim tomorrow. By practicing your turns, you can! Think about that. Most swimmers start at 1.6 seconds per turn. By the end of one practice, most are down to .8. That adds up to 2.4 seconds over the length of a 100. Coach X strongly encourages you to do this experiment and practice your turns until you can get them consistently under 1.0 second each.

TIP: Practice all of your turns for each stroke until you can do them all in under one second. Most swimmers can do this in a single practice and drop 2.4 seconds in their next 100 yard swim!

SIGHTING THE TURNS

Have you ever noticed those strange markings on the bottom of the pool? Every pool has them, but when Coach X asks swimmers what they are for, almost no one knows! Did you ever wonder why the lines on the bottom don't go all the way to the wall? It turns out it is deliberate and they always end exactly the same distance from the wall in every pool. They are, in fact, down there to make you faster!

Pretty much every swimmer is familiar with the purpose of the backstroke flags. When looking straight up, you swim under the flags and you know there are a set number of strokes until you reach the wall. Without looking for the wall, you count your strokes, do your turn and streamline away. The same is true for the targets at the bottom of the pool.

By looking straight down you are able to see the target on the bottom without the need to lift your head during a turn. Just as with the backstroke flags, every swimmer will have a certain stroke count from the moment they spot the target. All you need to do is figure out what your count is and then you will never have to lift your head on a turn again. Simply look straight down, count your strokes when you pass the target, do your turn, and streamline away. Your turns will be significantly faster when you look down and use the target!

TIP: Never look for the wall! Use the target on the bottom of the pool the same way you use the backstroke flags. Know your stroke count!

HEADS UP

Is it okay to lift your head up to sight for the wall before or during a turn? Simply put, don't do it! When going into the wall for a turn you want to make sure that you have full power. This means that you should *not* be gliding into a turn. You need to kick, get your speed up and carry that speed through the rotation. The moment you lift your head out of the water, your hips are going to sink and as we've learned, this is the equivalent of pulling the hand brake in a car. Never take a breath when doing into a turn. It's just the wrong thing to do.

TIP: Never take a breath as you execute a turn. Lifting your head changes your hip position and slows you down! If you really need a breath take one and only one breath as you pass the flags.

HUNTER'S STORY

This is the story of a swimmer named Hunter. Like most of the swimmers in this book he was one of the faster kids on his team. At age thirteen he already had his Junior Olympic times in almost every event. Hunter was very close to getting his Far Western Qualifying times. In fact he had been trying to get his times down for several weeks in all the strokes, but none more so than his 100 meter butterfly.

Hunter was a great athlete and he listened to everything his coach told him to do. In an attempt to get his time down, Hunter's coach decided to move him into a new group. The new group trained two times a day for a total of four hours, plus he now trained on the weekends. After about one month of swimming with the new group Hunter was convinced that he would finally get his Far Western times at the next meet.

The day finally arrived and Hunter was absolutely determined not only to get his Far Western time, but to win his heat and take first place overall. When the buzzer went off he flew off the block like a superhero! He was out in front in a heartbeat and kept his lead all the way to the first wall. As he came off the turn he noticed in his peripheral vision that he had lost his lead.

It was not by much and so he dug in and pushed hard, recovering his hands low and fast with straight arms. By the middle of the pool Hunter slowly crept back into the lead. He saw the wall up ahead and knew that he would make this turn his fastest ever. Pushing harder and harder he focused on the wall planning his turn.

As he pushed off, again he was shocked to find himself no longer in first place. In fact, this time he had slipped all the way into third! Hunter became desperate to make sure that he would smoke his competition on the third and final turn. By this time his body was starting to hurt and it was getting harder and harder to force his hands forward. He was getting tired and he knew it, but he was not going to let that stop him from nailing this final turn.

Hunter threw everything he had into the turn, pushed off, undulated with fast strong body dolphins, did a perfect pull down and was sure that he had come out in first place. But he hadn't. He was back to third. Wanting his time now more than ever, he was nearly crying. He reached inside himself and focused on the finish. He saw the wall ahead and pushed harder and harder and harder, pulling up to the other swimmers in his heat. His eyes were glued on the finish and as he touched he prayed that he had got his Far Western time. Hunter tore off his now tear filled goggles to look up at the score board. He had come in third place and added nearly three seconds to his best time!

When Hunter went to talk to his coach about the race, Hunter's parents brought over a video they had just shot of the swim. The coach asked Hunter what he thought happened to slow him down. Unfortunately Hunter did not know; he thought he did everything correctly and told his coach that he was very focused on the turns but they just always seemed to be slow for some reason.

The coach reviewed the video with Hunter and showed him that it was Hunter's focus on the turns that was his undoing. At each turn, instead of tucking his head and looking for the target at the bottom of the pool, Hunter got excited and started to lift his head and sight the wall above water. This in turn lowered his hips and created extra drag. The other swimmers in the heat kept their heads down and as a result got into the turn faster. At each wall the effect was increased because Hunter continued to become increasingly desperate, sighting the wall earlier and earlier.

This is a very common mistake for swimmers trying to reach a goal time. Learn from Hunter's swim and remember that when you are trying to reach a goal, it is critical that you not sight your turns and do not look for the walls!

TRIPLE LINDY

There is a movie which Coach X enjoys very much. It is an older movie starring the late comedian Rodney Dangerfield. Rodney was not at all a slim man. In fact, he plays the owner of a big and fat store in this movie. He also happens to play the role of one of the world's greatest divers. During one of the final scenes of the movie Rodney is called in to help his son's college win a diving competition. To complete his dive, Rodney has a third diving board installed so that he can perform his world famous dive: The Triple Lindy. The dive is hilarious as Rodney bounces from board to board in a very loose and wide legged tuck. While the form looks terrible the dive itself is absolutely spectacular. Rodney did the loose leg tuck for comedic effect, but in reality, he may have been on to something.

FEET PLACEMENT FOR TURNS

Since we enjoy experiments so much, Coach X has another one for you. It's pretty easy too! All you need to do is jump. If possible, have a friend measure how high you can jump off the ground while doing these various tests. For the first jump, go ahead and jump with your legs and feet together (the same way most swimmers place their legs while doing a turn).

For the second jump, start with your feet at shoulder width apart, jump and bring your legs and feet together after the push. Which of these jumps got you higher in the air? Chances are it was the second jump! Wow!

To find out why this is so incredible, just watch any age group swimming meet. Nearly every swimmer in the pool is dutifully squeezing their legs and feet together when hitting the wall. I say dutifully because it seems that most coaches out there have been telling their age group swimmers to keep their legs together when going into a turn. I bet those same coaches don't make their swimmers jump off of a starting block like that! So why would they be telling you to do it off the wall? Coach X certainly doesn't know.

So, if you find that you can jump higher on the second jump of the experiment, Coach X recommends that you hit the wall with your feet at shoulder width when doing any push offs or turns. If your coach asks what you are doing you can say that you are practicing for a Triple Lindy. If your coach wants more details, just do the experiment as a demonstration. If the coach yells at you... well – you'd best just listen or find a new coach.

TIP: Keep your feet and legs shoulder width apart when doing a turn! Never place your feet and legs together when pushing off a wall on a turn.

HULA HANDS OR ICE CREAM EATERS

Over the years Coach X has traveled many places and worked with many different coaches. He has heard some very unique ways of explaining what to do with the hands during an open turn. Descriptions like, "answer the telephone", "Eat some ice cream", "Do the hula", and "Be like Timmy" (referring to the boy in the movie Jurassic Park that climbs an electric fence.). There are a lot of ways to describe the arms, but what is the best way to actually move them? Many swimmers and coaches feel that the best way is for one arm to come over the head. Others feel the best way is to simply twist the body and to keep both the arms at water level. Whenever there is more than one way to do something, it is always a good idea to throw some science at it.

ICE CAPADES

Again, an experiment is in order. This time however, we are going to mix in a little bit of physics to go with it. One rule of physics is that when the arms are closer to the body it is much easier to spin quickly. This is known as the conservation of angular momentum. Yes, that is just as cool as it sounds! Think of an ice skater going into a spin. They start slowly with their arms extended, and then as they bring their arms in closer to their body they begin to spin so quickly that they become only a blur. So, from purely an observational standpoint it seems to be faster to spin (or turn) when the arms are closer to the body. Let's do an experiment and see.

SPINNING CHAIR OF DEATH

For this experiment we get to become dizzy! Give it a try, but first select a nice soft place in case you fall or crash into. This experiment should be done on a chair that can spin in a full circle. Please do not overdo it with this experiment! Yes, every middle school age swimmer – I am talking to you!

Go ahead and start spinning in circles with your arms extended. Do a few rotations and get a feel for the speed. Next do the same experiment and begin to pull your arms in to your body. Watch what happens to your rotational speed.

Now it's true that when you do a turn in the water you are not exactly spinning in circles, but in some ways you are. Give it a try in the water. When you do an open turn, rather than allowing one hand to come over your head, try pulling both arms in very close to your body. Spin, and then shoot both hands forward in a streamline. See if this makes you noticeably faster.

If it does, stick to it. If it doesn't, give it a few more tries to make sure that you've got it right. If it still doesn't help, go back to your old way. Not every technique is going to work for every swimmer. We are all unique and who knows, you may have found a superior method for your particular needs.

TIP: Keep your elbows and hands in tight to your body when doing an open turn to dramatically increase your turn speed!

TURN TIP SUMMARY

TIP: Practice all of your turns for each stroke until you can do them all in under one second. Most swimmers can do this in a single practice and drop 2.4 seconds in their next 100 yard swim!

TIP: Never look for the wall! Use the target on the bottom of the pool the same way you use the backstroke flags. Know your stroke count!

TIP: Never take a breath as you execute a turn. Lifting your head changes your hip position and slows you down! If you really need a breath take one and only one breath as you pass the flags.

TIP: Keep your feet and legs shoulder width apart when doing a turn! Never place your feet and legs together when pushing off a wall on a turn.

TIP: Keep your elbows and hands in tight to your body when doing an open turn to dramatically increase your turn speed!

FINISHES

"In theory there is no difference between theory and practice. In practice there is."

Yogi Berra

FINISHES

It's the last thing that most swimmers think about; literally. Swimmers spend hours each day practicing their strokes, working in yardage to improve aerobic thresholds, vital lung capacity and breathing patterns. They spend hours working on the perfect start and perhaps just as much time working on turns. Then at the meet they execute. The perfect start, the perfect race, the perfect turn, and the perfect second place finish. All because they didn't train for the last few yards of the race; the finish!

ELIJAH'S STORY

On a team on the East Coast, Coach X had the opportunity to work with a teenage swimmer named Elijah. He was known as one of the fastest breaststroke swimmers on his team. In fact, he was one of the fastest breaststroke swimmers period. The problem was that he almost never came in first place.

Elijah's parents came to Coach X because Elijah was getting very close to a reportable time in his local swimming committee (LSC). That is to say, he was approaching a place in the top sixteen swimmers in his area. However, as the deadline to achieve the time for his age group decreased, Elijah's times were increasing! His parents were desperate.

Coach X happened to be in the area and agreed to watch Elijah swim during one of his meets. In addition, the family routinely videotaped each of Elijah's events and was able to provide the footage to Coach X. Upon watching the videos and the live race, it was immediately evident to Coach X what was going on.

Elijah dove into the pool and had an awesome start. He was able to get out nearly halfway during the initial pull down. When he broke the surface he was already half a body length ahead of the next fastest swimmer. As the race progressed, a few of the other swimmers caught him and even passed him until they came to the turn. Elijah had a fast turn and a great underwater breakout. He easily regained his lead. Going into the last 50 meters of the race, Elijah was clearly in front by at least a full body length.

At the halfway point he was keeping his head low and had a fantastic glide that was keeping him out in front. As he passed the halfway point on the final length he took a breath and glanced up at the flags. Elijah knew that he had to drop a second to make it to the top sixteen listings. He saw the flags and knew what he had to do. Elijah dug in and gave it everything he had. He did not for one second take his eye off the prize: The wall at the end of the lane.

As he turned on the power and speed and started to feel the pain, he noticed the swimmers in the other lane were now neck and neck with him. With each stroke he would look left, then right and see the other swimmers pulling ahead. In the last few seconds of the race, Elijah went from a full body length ahead of everyone to a fourth place finish. What happened?

Some of you already know a few of the obvious issues that were described in Elijah's story. For example, at the end of the race, Elijah was looking at the competition. That meant that he wasn't focusing on his stroke technique. Generally this results in shorter strokes with a slower stroke cycle. The result is a considerably slower race time.

Elijah's coach had picked up on that problem, but what everyone seemed to miss was the blazingly obvious problem that Coach X saw. Elijah wanted to win so badly, wanted to drop time so much, that he completely focused on the finish wall. Up to that point his head was down in the water and he was gliding. As soon as he saw the wall, he would keep his head up out of the water and focus on the wall because that's where he wanted to go. But by lifting his head up to look at the wall he was slamming the brakes on his stroke! As he slowed down he would look at the wall more and more until his head never went back into the water. It was a vicious cycle that acted to slow down Elijah's swims so much that he often added time.

When Coach X pointed this out to Elijah using the videotape of his race it was instantly obvious to everyone. The next meet, Elijah forced himself to look straight at the bottom and to look for the 'T' that marks the end of the lane at the bottom of the pool. When he saw this he did one last push and touched the wall for a two second time drop! He made the top sixteen!

TEA TIME AT THE POOL

When doing clinics around the world, Coach X likes to ask the swimmers a very simple question: "What is the 'T' at the bottom of each lane there for?" You would think that after looking at it lap after lap every single day, that every swimmer would raise their hand with the correct answer. The reality is that when Coach X asks this question, very rarely does anyone ever answer, and when they do, it's usually wrong.

The interesting thing is that if Coach X asks the question, "Why are the backstroke flags there?" Everyone puts up their hand, and everyone is right. Yes, the 'T' at the bottom of the pool is supposed to serve exactly the same purpose as the backstroke flags but for all three other strokes. That means you should be making use of the 'T' seventy-five percent more time than the backstroke flags. So why do so many swimmers have no idea what they are for? Because very few swimmers ever practice finishes correctly!

TIP: Never look at the finish! Use the 'T' at the bottom of the pool and know your stroke count.

Whenever you race and especially whenever you practice you should *never* be lifting your head out of the water on a finish – period! The black 'T' at the bottom of the pool is there to tell you that you are getting close so that you don't have to lift your head. Just as you have a count from the flags to the wall for backstroke, so too should you have a count in each of your strokes from the 'T' to the wall. This will allow you to spot the 'T', turn on that extra super burst of power at the end and touch the wall, all without ever lifting your head. Remember that lifting your head even a small amount will slow you down and that's *not* what you want at the end of the race.

FAR REACHING

It's about time for another experiment. This is a fun one. Okay, well they are all fun, but this one you don't even need to enter the pool to try.

FAR REACHING

Stand in front of a wall and turn to face it directly. You will want to stand an arm's length away from the wall so that the fingertips of both hands just barely touch the wall. Now, backup exactly one pace by placing one foot behind the other, toe to heel. If you do this correctly your fingertips should now be about two of your feet away from the wall. Get ready for the amazing part. Rotate your body by keeping your feet still and twisting at the waist. You will discover that your fingertips now exactly touch the wall!

The point of this experiment is to teach you that, how most swimmers finish a race, is probably the slowest possible way to finish. Go ahead and watch a few races at your local swim meet. You will see that almost all of the swimmers in the slower heats all finish on their stomach or on their back in front crawl and in backstroke. As you've just discovered, it's actually possible to reach the wall about a foot or two sooner simply by rolling to your side. This is *extremely* valuable information!

Winning a race comes down to split seconds. If you are exactly tied with the person in the next lane and you roll to extend your arm on the finish, while your opponent finishes flat on their stomach or back, guess who's going to win. Here's a hint: it won't be them!

TIP: Always finish by reaching on your side in front crawl or backstroke! You will outreach and out touch your competition and win the race.

TIMING IS EVERYTHING

For breaststroke and butterfly, the finish is all in the timing. Coach X cannot tell you how many times he's seen a swimmer lose a race because they took an extra stroke within inches of the wall. You will be much better off getting your head completely under the arms, stretching with everything you've got, squeezing your butt muscles, overlapping your toes and then powering with your kick. Remember in both butterfly and breast it is *not* required that you breathe. As long as some part of your head is breaking the surface on the finish, even if it is the size of a quarter, you will be legal.

TIP: If the wall is further than an arm's length away, never take the extra stroke.

By becoming more streamlined you will reduce your drag into the finish. Taking an extra stroke will take too much time and within one arm's length you will have forward momentum. This means that you wouldn't be able to get in a full arm stoke and you would finish with your arms in a strange position too close to the wall.

Ideally, you should practice your stroke so that you can finish the race with your fingertips just touching the wall with a fully extended arm. Use the 'T' at the bottom of the pool to adjust your timing until you get it perfect each time. Finishing at the wall at full arm length is critical to getting the best time possible.

CLEAR PROP!

Another very common mistake that Coach X observes at swimming meets is watching a swimmer glide to the finish. Bad, bad, bad! These are the most critical moments of the race. There should be absolutely nothing slowing the swimmer down at this point. It is absolutely critical that the swimmer is going at full force speed into the wall. This is why many backstroke swimmers now finish with a body dolphin as using the abdominal muscles allows for a much more powerful burst of speed at the end; just remember to keep your toes above the surface!

When finishing in other strokes, ensure that you are fully powered. Your kick should be the strongest as you break the 'T' point in the lane. In addition to power, pour in the speed. That kick rate should be beyond "white water" as you come into the finish. Just remember to push water with your kick and not air. In short, you need to propel your body at top speed using your kick.

TIP: Never glide into a finish! Always power to the final wall; kick as hard as possible and do everything you can to provide extra propulsion.

DO NOT GO GENTLE INTO THAT WALL

Knowing that they should not take an extra stroke causes many swimmers to make another type of mistake. As it turns out, it is the exact same mistake that many novice martial art students make when first learning to break a board with their hand. Instinctively, someone without training will attempt to strike the board with all of their force directed at the front surface. This is exactly the wrong thing to do. If you try this you will end up with a very sore hand and a very unbroken board. To break the board you need to direct your force *through* the board. In other words, don't stop your hand at the front surface; instead imagine your hand going all the way through the board and out the other side.

Why is learning to break a board relevant to swimming? Because if you try to time finishes so that your fingertips just touch the wall on the last stroke, chances are you are not using all of your power. In swimming, power equals speed. Simply put, by not imagining your hand going through the wall, you are slowing it down to make the touch!

TIP: Finish as if directing your hand six inches through the wall. Pretending the actual finish is through the wall ensures you maintain full speed at the touch.

PUNCHING IN

Here is another mistake that Coach X has seen many times. Oddly this one seems to play out in many movies that involve swimming. Apparently Hollywood thinks that it is more dramatic for the winning swimmer to punch the wall during the finish. This probably came about from the fist-pump in other sports, but Coach X assures you, this is *not* a good idea in swimming.

Coach X recently had the pleasure of viewing a movie with a local swim team. The movie is about a boy who helps a wounded dolphin get a new tail. During one scene in the movie the fastest swimmer is doing front crawl and the camera switches to an underwater view where we see the lead swimmer "slap" the wall for the finish. Coach X was pleased to hear audible gasps of disgust from the swimmers in the audience. They knew that was no way to finish!

TIP: Keep the arm pumps until after the race, never punch or slap the wall during a finish!

FINISHES TIP SUMMARY

TIP: Never look at the finish! Use the 'T' at the bottom of the pool and know your stroke count.

TIP: Always finish by reaching on your side in front crawl or backstroke! You will outreach and out touch your competition and win the race.

TIP: If the wall is further than an arm's length away, never take the extra stroke.

TIP: Never glide into a finish! Always power to the final wall; kick as hard as possible and do everything you can to provide extra propulsion.

TIP: Finish as if directing your hand six inches through the wall.   Pretending the actual finish is through the wall ensures you maintain full speed at the touch.

TIP: Keep the arm pumps until after the race, never punch or slap the wall during a finish!

STROKES

"Every great and deep difficulty bears in itself its own solution. It forces us to change our thinking in order to find it."

Niels Bohr

STROKE SCIENCE

A lot of research has gone into understanding the four basic strokes of competitive swimming. In the United States there are centers dedicated to studying the world's fastest swimmers to understand what makes them fast. While this is a noble cause, one still needs to stop for a moment and take a step back and look at the bigger picture.

Throughout Coach X's many years of coaching he has seen many a swimmer look up to an Olympian, longing to be just like that Olympian. Having mentors is a very good thing. They often can help us reach our goals by giving us something we aspire to be. But, be very cautious about studying Olympians and be very cautious about trying to swim exactly like this swimmer or that. Coach X personally knows of several excellent swimming coaches and authors who write a new book on swimming just about every four years. Why every four years? Because they watch the Olympics, see how the new record holders swam and then write books telling you that this is how it should be done.

TIP: Avoid reading swimming books that are printed right after the Olympics.

Here is the problem with this approach. If you aspire to do everything exactly like your favorite Olympian, as great as he or she may be, then you will NEVER be better than them. The fact of the matter is that every Olympian has stroke flaws. This sometimes comes as a huge surprise to many swimmers who idolize the Olympians and believe them to be perfect. They are not. Usually they will be the first to tell you this. Sometimes their "flaw" is part of what makes them unique, so for that swimmer it works; but *not* for 99.999% of the world. So if you do everything exactly as they do, you will develop the exact same stroke flaws. If you duplicate that one technique that only works for that swimmer, you are only going to worsen your times. What you need to do is find the things that really are making them fast and do only those things.

TIP: If you do exactly what your favorite Olympian does, you will NEVER become better than them.

But, figuring out what these things are can often be much harder than you might think. First is the issue of swimming being an art as much as it is a science. How do you know what works for the Olympian and for you as well? Then there is the issue of fitting science to meet expectations. This is a very bad trap that many people fall into. Those who do not follow the scientific method will often make an observation they believe to be true, then create data to support their idea and throw away data that does not. Let Coach X be very, very clear on this practice – it is *Not Science!*

TIP: Every Olympic athlete has stroke flaws. Duplicating how they swim may actually make you slower!

SCIENCE BASED SWIMMING

In real science there is a method that must be followed. We must start with a hypothesis, what we believe to be true. We must then create experiments, generally with at least two groups of people. One group has no changes at all, they just keep going the same as always and this group is the control. In the other group we make one single change that we can observe. Next we collect data. We cannot discard anything. If in the end the data disproves our hypothesis this information can still be useful, and more often than not, this is exactly what happens. Sometimes the data we collect does support our hypothesis and then we can construct more experiments to further investigate and further improve our knowledge and understanding. It's very hard work and it has to be that way. There simply cannot be any guess work in science. And that is the beauty of it. When you are done you are left with what works; not because someone believes it does, but because it actually does.

Here is a fantastic example of a very well-known coach and very well-known Olympic swimmer that failed to properly follow the scientific method and caused swimmers even to this very day to learn an incorrect stroke technique. Pseudo-science can be extremely dangerous, and the misinformation it spreads can last for decades. Coach X does not fault anyone for the analysis you are about to read. Everyone was acting in the best interest of swimmers at large; this is an example of a learning experience.

PSEUDO SCIENCE AND THE OLYPIAN

There is a very good story about a former Olympian who is now quite famous. His coach was pioneering in the analysis of swimming strokes and what made each of them fast. One day the coach and swimmer were asked, what makes this particular Olympic swimmer not just the fastest in the world but the best Olympian in history (at that time). The Olympian answered that he just pulls his arm straight back through the water. His coach immediately said, "No, no. He doesn't do that at all. We have the data in the computer. What he really does is swim by making an 'S' with his hand."

The coach explained he placed sensors on the swimmer that were recorded by a computer. While watching the image on the computer, the coach believed he saw the Olympian's hand move in an 'S' pattern on the screen. The problem with this research was that the coach did not start with a hypothesis and he did not actually collect any data to verify his hypothesis. Instead, he did the analysis in reverse. He simply collected data and then tried to pull something meaningful from it. This is what most people do when they write swimming books every four years. It is a very bad idea and the conclusions gained are almost always pseudo-science.

So for many, many years, swimmers doing front crawl were taught to swim by making an 'S' pattern. Many years later we realized that the Olympic swimmer's description, not the coach's, was correct. The Olympian was in fact simply pulling straight back; but, he

60

was rotating his body as he did this. If you take rotation into account, the 'S' is really a flattened out corkscrew. In other words, there never was an 'S', it was always a rotation, in conjunction with a straight pull backward. But because this swimmer was so ahead of his time, the coach didn't realize that this was the case. As a result, for nearly three decades, most swimmers were actually hurting their strokes in an effort to be like the world's fastest swimmer.

If the coach had first said, I believe this swimmer uses an 'S' pull he could have devised several experiments to test this hypothesis. He could have analyzed the data in three dimensions, rather than the flattened out two dimensions of the computer screen; which changed a rotation to an 'S'. He could have had the swimmer perform the stroke both with and without an 'S' to see if it made a difference in time. Because he only looked at data and then tried to pull something meaningful after the fact, his conclusion was wrong.

THREE MORE EXAMPLES OF WHY NOT TO IMITATE OLYMPIANS

Still not convinced that merely imitating Olympic athletes may not be a good idea? Coach X has several stories to share. Here are a few more quick examples:

Many years back a very famous backstroke swimmer won Olympic gold and soon everyone was doing a back flop into the water and swimming flat on their back. While the entry was soon discontinued due to the sheer pain it caused, the flat back backstroke endured for decades. Once swimmers figured out the benefit of rotation world records were again shattered.

In another year a "new" form of breaststroke began when one of the female swimmers started recovering with her hands out of the water. Very quickly all the breaststrokers around the world began trying to duplicate her technique. But a few years later swimmers began to realize that they were going slower and slower. It was not her hand recovery technique that made her fast. It was something else entirely. And yet again nearly a decade of swimmers suffered poorer times for it. If you had picked up any book by one of the top coaches at the time, this is exactly how they would tell you to swim.

Still not satisfied? Here's another more recent example. In the 2000 Olympic Games in Sydney, a gold medalist swam the 200 free without kicking for most of it. The underwater work showed that he did not kick at all for the entire first 100 meters, and then poured it on for the second half of the 200 to win. It was very impressive! Many aspiring swimmers saw this footage and began to duplicate it. Did they do any research to find out why the Olympian didn't kick during the first 100 meters? Was he sick? Did he get a cramp? Was it intentional? Who knows, but as a solid rule of science, the legs do act as a source of propulsion and by not kicking you may be saving energy, but at the expense of speed.

ONE MORE EXAMPLE FOR GOOD MEASURE

Recently during a *Science Based Swimming Clinic,* a student asked the best suit to wear while training. In general Coach X is a big fan of always training in the same type of suit that you use for competition. In other words if you will be wearing briefs for your races, then you should wear briefs at practice. Someone then asked a question about drag suits to which Coach X replied, "normally I don't mention this during a clinic because I only have one study, but it was a fairly large study and the bottom line was: Swimmers that wore drag suits were statistically slower after one season of training versus those who did not." Now Coach X does not particularly like how this study was done but it involved over 400 college athletes and deserves some attention when the question is asked. However, from the back of the room an Olympic athlete shouted out, "That's a complete lie!"

The Olympian then went on to say that he wore a drag suit the entire season leading up to the 2012 Summer Olympics and he competed in the Olympic Games. Coach X replied, attempting to be nice, "Yes, and according to the science you would have gone faster if you hadn't worn a drag suit during practice." The Olympian insisted this was nonsense, so Coach X asked the question, "By the way, where is your medal?" As it turned out he did not have a medal. At this, all the students in the classroom looked at the Olympic athlete and understood that even Olympian's are humans. The few hundredths of a second he may have added by training in a drag suit may very well have cost him medaling at the Olympics!

DON'T BE AN "ANEC-DOLT"

Fortunately Coach X was able to use this situation to teach a very important lesson. As human beings we are most influenced by our own experiences and those of people we either know or aspire to be like. Marketers really count on this. It is how they are able to sell you silly things like "power" bracelets to improve your balance, or special magnets to improve your performance. All of these things are nonsense, they don't work, so don't waste your money. But even having read that, if even one person you know comes up to you and says that it worked for them, you are more likely to believe your friend than twenty scientific studies that prove the opposite. In short, humans are hard wired to believe in anecdotes over science. Don't be an "anec-dolt"; believe the science.

TIP: Do not believe something works simply because someone you know tells you it does.

BOGUS BODY SUITS

Here is another example of how manufacturers convince swimmers that something works when it doesn't. Prior to the 2000 Sydney Olympics, full body suits were all the rage. Coach X has a personal friend who is an Olympian who was asked to try out some suits for a particular manufacturer and post what he thought about them. The manufacturer gave him suit #1 and said it should make him a little faster. He tried it and reported that he did indeed feel faster. They gave him suit #2 and said this will make you even a little faster. He tried it and he reported that he felt even faster. Then they gave him suit #3 and they said this would make him feel super-fast. He tried it, and he reported feeling super-fast.

Many, many swimmers follow this particular person and they really trust what he has to say. The problem is, even if he was right and he did feel faster, it is only an anecdote. It's one person's experience. As it turned out Coach X had been doing some research into these particular suits and found no less than twenty-seven independent studies which indicated that they did not perform as described. Further, Coach X actually sought out the designer of these suits to interview them for this book.

It took many years to get the interview, but finally Coach X scored! He actually sat down with the CEO of one of the top suit manufacturers in the country. Unfortunately the CEO refused to go on record officially, so Coach X cannot reveal the source. However, he admitted that the body suits prior to the 2000 Olympics were a complete sham. They simply did not work. The manufacturers simply relied on Olympic and elite level athletes to spread the word that they worked to sell more suits at a greater profit margin. Seriously! He even told me that, "if they think it works and it works for them, then what's the harm?"

TIP: In almost all situations the fastest competition suit is actually a brief! Nearly all independent studies show that jammers are, in general, the slowest of all suits.

WHAT'S THE HARM?

When a pharmaceutical company is trying to create a new drug they must prove that it works better than a placebo. What is a placebo? It is a fake copy of the thing they are trying to prove works. For example, say someone developed a pill to cure cancer. They would create a placebo by making an identical pill out of saw dust. They would then get 100 people together, giving half of them the cancer cure pill and half of them the saw dust pill. The remarkable thing is that a certain number of people getting the saw dust pill will still recover from their cancer! However, it was not the pill that did it. That is why the cancer pill must prove that it works significantly better than the saw dust pill.

Just imagine if this was not the case. Someone badly needing that cancer cure pill may be friends with the person who recovered using the saw dust pill. Hearing this, they decide to take a saw dust pill to cure their cancer; and they die.

Unfortunately there are no such standards in swimming. Any manufacturer can sell you absolutely anything and make pretty much any claim about it that they want. In the case of body suits, any manufacturer could use the worst material they had in stock just to get rid of it, sew it into a body suit and tell a swimmer it will make them fast. They could then sell that suit for over $1,000.00. Someone would but it and because the manufacturer told them it will make them faster, they may believe it and actually go a little faster. The problem is, that swimmer could have gone just as fast in any other suit; probably faster in regular briefs, and they would have saved nearly $1,000.00 in the process. That is the harm. Cheating people out of their money for a product that does not really do what it claims to do.

In fact if you have an opportunity, watch some of the faster boys races at an age group meet. At least in California, you will notice something fascinating. The young, slow, swimmers usually always have jammers. As the boys get older and faster they start wearing briefs. In the fastest heats the boys wearing briefs almost always beat the boys wearing jammers. Often times less skilled swimmers will purchase an expensive jammer to be fast, but the great swimmers just wear technical briefs and crush the guys with the expensive jammers.

So please, heed Coach X's warning. Don't listen to your friends or to the manufacturers. Do the science, do the research. Find out what independent studies show and ignore the studies funded by the manufacturers. Why? Well, according to nearly every study ever done by the tobacco industry there is no link between smoking and cancer. Think about that, then decide if you really want to trust studies funded by the suit manufacturer.

TIP: Always use a placebo test to see if a claim is valid.

42 (THE ANSWER TO EVERYTHING)

So what are we to do if we can't trust the Olympians? The answer really isn't all that hard. This is exactly the sort of thing that scientific analysis can excel at, and this is why science is the fundamental basis of this book. Here we will show you how to go fast based on the latest scientific understanding. Keep in mind that we are learning something new every single day and what is presented here now may not be the same in the future.

There is at least one fabulous website out there (www.goswim.tv) that will allow you to view many Olympic swimmers and you may be surprised to learn that Coach X actually supports this site. This is because, if you know the science behind your stroke, this site makes it easy to find incredible examples of Olympic athletes doing these exact techniques. In fact there is another site Coach X recommends (strokelab.finisinc.com) which will let you watch your own videos side by side with the Olympic videos from goswim! By watching those specific videos you can become a *Super Sprinter*, and what's great is that if you happen to fit the rule of thumbs, you can almost certainly find a video of an Olympic swimmer who happens to share your particular mutation. It's a great site and Coach X highly recommends it. But if you want to use that site, you first need to know what to look for. So, if you want to be the fastest swimmer you can be today… read on.

STROKE SCIENCE TIP SUMMARY

TIP: Avoid reading swimming books that are printed right after the Olympics.

TIP: If you do exactly what your favorite Olympian does, you will NEVER become better than them.

TIP: Every Olympic athlete has stroke flaws. Duplicating how they swim may actually make you slower!

TIP: Do not believe something works simply because someone you know tells you it does.

TIP: Compete in briefs! In almost all situations the fastest competition suit is actually a brief! Nearly all independent studies show that jammers are, in general, the slowest of all suits.

TIP: Always use a placebo test to see if a claim is valid.

FRONT CRAWL

"Many of life's failures are people who did not realize how close they were to success when they gave up."
Thomas A. Edison

FRONT CRAWL

SLIP SLIDING AWAY

Front crawl, or freestyle for those who do not know why it isn't, is hands down the most popular of all the competitive swimming strokes. Just look at any age group swimming meet. You will always find the most heats in the 50 Free. Why? Because the 50 Free is the only time you are allowed to swim Front Crawl. Sure you could swim butterfly or backstroke or even breast during the 50 freestyle, but not many would. Because there are so many swimmers in this event it becomes terribly important that you use absolutely everything available to you to improve your time. But before you go looking for that elite sprint suit, and spend hundreds of dollars, maybe you should start with your stroke?

By far, this chapter on front crawl is going to be the most difficult to write and it is sure to be one of the most controversial. There are many, many very fast swimmers that don't practice a single thing that we are going to talk about. How do they do it? Mostly by using pure muscle. But the problem with this approach is that while it may work well for a year or two, most swimmers can't keep up the muscle needed to keep dropping times as they age up. The result is that many swimmers get discouraged and either switch strokes or give up all together. Coach X doesn't want to see that happen to you! So in this chapter we are going to try to answer many of the little questions that you might have about what makes you go fast in front crawl and what will slow you down.

LAPS, LAPS AND MORE LAPS

One approach to improving your time is to simply train harder. This is almost always a good idea. But the problem is most people *only* train harder, they never train smarter. Let's think about racing a single 25 yards of front crawl. Let's say that you are a young swimmer, fairly new to the sport and you currently swim it in 15 seconds. When your friends ask you for your time, you would tell them, "I can swim a 25 free in 15 seconds." But what if your friend asked you how fast you were going at the first set of flags? What about at the 12 ½ yard mark? Would you know your speed? Probably not. This is because most swimmers never think about their instantaneous rate of speed (how fast was I moving at a given point), they only think about their average rate of speed (how long did it take me to go a certain distance). In truth you are never really swimming the entire length at exactly 15 seconds / 25 yards. You are in fact speeding up and slowing down through the entire race.

TIP: Your speed in a race is never constant. Learning to be slippery during a recovery can improve your overall time as much as three months of hard training!

This is easy to imagine if you consider your times during a 100 yard race. The first length is usually very fast, the second is generally a little slower, the third length is often the slowest, and then in the last length you speed up again. Not only does this sort of thing happen every length, it is actually happening during every stroke! Think about how you move in the water. When you start the pull, you force water behind you, making you increase your speed as you move forward. As you recover your arms, you are gliding and slowing down. So as you swim you are speeding up and slowing down with every stroke you take.

If you've never thought of that before, don't feel bad. Most coaches haven't given it too much thought either. But this fact is one of the most important things in all of swimming. Why? Let me explain.

Going back to our example of the swimmer doing 25 yards in 15 seconds; let's say the swimmer really wants to go faster. The swimmer will ask his coach what he can do to improve his speed. The coach will train the swimmer by increasing the yardage, working the swimmer harder so his body can increase oxygen intake and muscle efficiency, and put him on a weight program to increase his body strength. This swimmer will follow this program for two hours in the morning, and two hours at night. Now let's say that the swimmer has to miss practice on Monday due to a holiday. It will likely take the swimmer all the way until Wednesday or Thursday before he is back to the place he was when he missed a single day. After several weeks the swimmer enters a meet, and because of his training he is now able to pull much harder on the water. As a result, his speed is slightly faster during the pull part of the stroke and his average speed for the 25 yard front crawl drops to a 13!

But, is there another way that the swimmer could have got that same time without training so hard? The answer, despite what many coaches would tell you, is absolutely yes! What if when the swimmer asked the coach to help him go faster and the coach did not increase the workout at all, but instead showed the swimmer ways to simply not slow down so much during the recovery or glide portions of the stroke. The swimmer would have gone to the same meet, and using absolutely NO more energy than last time, they would simply not slow down as much during the recovery. As a result, his speed during the recovery would be faster. The same swimmer would have dropped time and would be swimming a 25 front crawl in 13 seconds, but without using any extra effort at all! Does it sound amazing? Incredible? Impossible? The fact is, it is absolutely true! Most coaches simply either do not know about this, or they simply focus more on the physical aspects of the stroke and training. The point is, to be your best, you need to attack the problem in both ways.

TIP: Reducing drag during recovery costs no energy and will drop your times over 10%!

In this chapter Coach X is going to tell you what you need to know so that you can go faster during your recovery. But, I want to point out one very important thing. Training the pull and training the recovery do not cancel out! In other words, there is absolutely no reason that you cannot do both at once and drop even more time! In the example above, if the swimmer had trained to improve both his pull and his recovery, his new 25 front crawl time would have been an 11!

TIP: Train to improve both your physical stroke and reduce drag during your recovery to double your time drops!

MYTHS AND MISCONCEPTIONS

While explaining ways that you can keep your speed during your recovery, I will try to answer several myths and misconceptions about front crawl. For example, what about swimming with your fingers spread? What about flinging your arms instead of spearing into the water? How about reaching over the water as far as possible? What is more efficient – a windmill approach or a catch up type approach to arm entry? How much force can you put on the water during the pull before your hand begins to slip though the water with no power?

SPIDER MAN OR SWAMP THING

Fingers open or closed? Here is a great item for debate. You've probably seen many swimmers even on your own team pull their hand through the water with their fingers open. Some may even have entered the water like this. Is it faster? Of course not! How could it be? With your hand cupped you can get a much better grip on the water and a better pull. Or, maybe not. While having the fingers closed on the entry is a good idea, it may not be the best thing to do during the pull. Spreading your fingers slightly increases the width of your hand. In addition, opening the hand actually creates greater surface area. This means that there is more skin touching the water. Think of it as making your hand about twice as big as it would normally be. "Yes", you say, "but, if I open my fingers they will just slip through the water." That is of course true if you really spread your fingers apart a great distance. If you simply open your hand a little bit, you will still be able to put pressure on the water and get more surface area on the water. The more area that you can use for propulsive force with minimal drag, the faster you will go.

TIP: Do not squeeze your fingers firmly together when doing a pull. A very small amount of space is actually good as it widens the hand and creates more surface area during the pull.

WE ARE HERE TO PUMP YOU UP!

Some years back, Coach X was doing a swimming clinic at a high school in the Midwest where the local coach had all of the swimmers doing a very aggressive weight program. One of the swimmers came up to Coach X and bragged that he could bench press 200 pounds. Coach X asked the swimmer how that would help him during his swimming. The swimmer gave a very strange look as though it should be totally obvious and then he said that it meant he could pull harder on the water. Coach X asked him why he thought that would help him. He gave Coach X that strange look again and said that the harder you pull on the water the faster you go. Really?

Coach X bets that a lot of swimmers out there have been taught the same thing. But if that is what someone told you, they forgot about the laws of science. It turns out there is a limit to how much force you can apply to water before you stop getting an effective pull and you are spending more energy than you're getting back in speed. But there is also a law of physics that says that in order to put twice as much force on the water; you will need to provide four times as much energy. If you try to put four times as much force on the water it will require sixteen times as much energy. That's right – the amount of energy required isn't just doubled, it is the square of the force you are trying to achieve!

ERIC'S STORY

The swimmer in this story was named Eric. He was fifteen at the time and it was his second year on the high school swimming team. Eric's coach was a fairly seasoned guy who was not just the coach of the high school team, but also head coach for a year round age group team in the area. It turns out that Eric was currently swimming about a 1:15.00 in the 100 yard backstroke and his coach told him that by working the weights Eric would be able to swim a 100 yard backstroke in 1:00.00 by the end of the season. Keep in mind that through an aggressive weight lifting program, Eric was now bench pressing about 200 pounds several times a week. Let's break this down and see why the coach's plan for Eric was just plain crazy.

As we said, Eric can do the 100 back in about 1:15.00 seconds (75 seconds). He wants to improve his time over the three month season by 20% for a new best time of 1:00.00 (60 seconds).

Using force alone, Eric's goal would require him to apply 1.25 times more force on the water to attain his new speed:
(Current time: 75 seconds / goal time 60 seconds = 1.25 times faster.)

The energy required for Eric to increase his force on the water by 1.25 times is the square of that number; meaning you have to multiply it by itself:
(1.25 * 1.25 = 1.5625, but we will round it to 1.6 times as much energy to produce the required force on the water.)

Since his current power comes from his arm muscles through bench pressing 200 pounds; for Eric to produce enough power to drop to 1:00.00 he would have to bench press:
(200 pounds * 1.6 = 320 pounds!)

For most swimmers, trying to increase your bench weight from 200 to 320 pounds in three months is absolutely ridiculous! Even if it were possible, dropping additional time would require the same approach. In fact to drop just ten additional seconds would require Eric to bench over 450 pounds! You can see that neither he, nor the coach, really thought that one out very well.

When Coach X explained this concept during the clinic, neither the coach nor any of the swimmers would believe it. They insisted that this just did not make sense and they continued the aggressive weight training program. Unfortunately the coach did not focus too much on stroke technique and relied heavily on his weight program. The result was one of the worst athletic seasons in memory for the high school team and the coach was not asked to return the next year. In the end Eric did not reach his goal and was ultimately very frustrated with swimming. Fortunately he stuck with the sport and continued to improve through his senior year, although Coach X does not know if he ever did make his cut of 1:00.00 in the 100 yard backstroke.

Regardless of what we want to believe is true, science is science. There is no denying it. When the laws of physics say that the energy required is the square of the desired force, they mean it. Believing that this is not so will not make it go away. That is why basing all your strokes and practices in a scientifically founded way will ensure that you go great lengths without disappointment.

Still, having good body strength is an important part of becoming a *Super Sprinter*. Overall body fitness plays a very big role in your performance in the water. Strength training can be an important part of any swimming program, but as a *Super Sprinter* you need to know when someone is putting too much emphasis on weights and dry land training. Regardless of your amount of force on the water, it is important to get the most out of your pull. For this, it is important you remember to anchor your arm so that you do not slip through the water.

TIP: Never use weight training alone to improve your speed. The amount of weight needed is the square of the amount of force you need to apply on the water!

ANCHORING

Most swimmers recognize the importance of a good anchor even though most don't even know what it really is. For those that don't know what we are talking about, it is not tying a large heavy metal object to your body. Your coach may have explained it as positioning your arm in such a way as to get a good hold on the water. This is how most swimmers understand what it means to anchor during a swim, but few understand truly how important it really is. In fact it would probably surprise many swimmers to learn that 90% of the time they are actually swimming backwards due to a bad anchor! Swimming backwards? How is that possible?

SWIMMING BACKWARDS

"Swimming Backwards" occurs because the coach's definition doesn't explain what really happens during a good anchor. To most swimmers and coaches anchoring amounts to nothing more than grabbing the water and holding it before you pull your hand backward. However, once you truly understand what it means to anchor, you will quickly realize that there really is no pull in any stroke.

Instead each "pull" should be considered an anchor. Rather than trying to pull your arms and hands backward, you are really trying to hold that spot on the water and push your hips forward to the anchor position. A nice way to learn a good anchor is to use the pool ladder on the deck. Stand one arm length away from the ladder and perform a single stroke in the direction of the ladder. With the stroking hand, grab hold of the ladder and then pull your hips past the ladder. To someone watching from a distance, it will appear that you "pulled" your hand backwards, but in fact, you actually pushed your hips toward your hand! When you do the opposite (pull your hand toward your hips), you are actually swimming backwards. Because this concept is hard for some swimmers to understand, Coach X will give you an experiment so you can see the effect for yourself.

SWIMMING BACKWARDS

It is easy to see if you are one of those swimmers that suffer from swimming backwards. You can do this experiment with a friend, a coach on deck, or use a video camera. Coach X favors the video camera, because that way you will get a chance to see for yourself what you are doing. Let's use front crawl for our example. We will use the alternating color pattern of the lane line buoys to mark our position throughout the experiment. Simply swim a regular 25 yards and play back the video. Then follow along with this example:

Pretend for a moment that your hips have just passed the solid buoys just under the flags (often called the gut zone). As you begin your first stroke, your right hand begins to enter the water exactly two buoys past the flags. SNAP. Take a picture at the exact moment your hand enters the water. We will call this "Point A".

As you continue to swim, your left hand now enters the water. SNAP. Let's take another picture at the exact moment this hand enters the water. We will call this "Point B." Now, compare the two images.

If you are like most swimmers, get ready for a shock. You may notice that your hips never made it to "Point A" (the buoy past the flags where your right hand had entered the water). In other words, you did not anchor properly. Your hips did not catch up to the first point of entry. If you look very carefully at the video you will see that in relation to your hand entries, your hips are literally moving backward in the water!

TIP: Anchor properly by not pulling on your hand until your hips pass the point of hand entry.

RELATIVITY IN SWIMMING

Albert Einstein was one of the greatest thinkers of the modern time. His papers on relativity were ground breaking in our understanding of the Universe. Coach X knows these concepts can be really hard for many swimmers and coaches to understand. Relative motion is great science, but it can get a little confusing when you use it to talk about swimming. If it is still hard for you to see, then Coach X has another, more simple, every day example.

HOW MERGING TRAFFIC IS LIKE BAD SWIMMING

Imagine driving in a car during heavy traffic. In front of you is a large truck and you must get off the freeway in a few more exits. However, as you drive forward, cars keep pulling in front of you. Even though your overall movement is forward, you are slowly getting bumped further and further backward behind that truck.

Taking this example back to the pool, the truck represents the pace your body *should* be traveling at when you anchor properly. The cars moving between you and the truck represent backward movement caused by poor anchoring. When you fail to get your hips to the point of entry it's just like a car had slipped in between you and that truck to slow you down and push you backward. Poor anchoring can significantly slow you down and destroy your times.

THE HOLY GRAIL

Many swimmers may be familiar with the popular movie, "The DiVinci Code" in which it is alleged that Leonardo DiVinci created clues to lead people to the location of the Holy Grail. While the movie is fiction, Leonardo DiVinci was a very real person. He was one of the greatest painters, scientists and Renaissance men to have ever lived. Several hundred years ago, DiVinci was the first to understand and write about human anatomy and physiology. He imagined flying machines such as hang gliders and even helicopters. Di Vinci was centuries ahead of his time. He single handedly did more to advance science in his day than just about anyone.

We are fortunate that Di Vinci was not just an incredible scientist, but also an incredible painter. In one of his famous creations, Di Vinci drew a picture of a human body that demonstrates why your height from head to toe is exactly the same as the distance between your outstretched arms from fingertip to fingertip. In swimming, this knowledge has immense value! Why? Because it means that if you are able to anchor properly on each stroke, your maximum speed should be equal to one full body length per stroke cycle.

TIP: When anchoring properly, your speed should equal one full body length per stroke cycle.

This is because during each stroke cycle you are taking two strokes, each stroke is the length of one arm. Therefore, if you really stretch and reach and anchor properly you will have traveled exactly one body length. So, if you ever wondered if body length really matters in swimming speed, DiVinci figured that out for us hundreds of years ago, and the answer is a definite YES!

TIP: Body length matters in swimming! The longer your arms (not your body), the faster you will swim!

SUPER SPRINTER SECRET

Because anchors are so important to swimming fast, many of you are probably asking if there is some way that you can improve how you anchor. The answer is yes, and Coach X will give you not one but two Super Sprinter secrets to make your anchors rock!

First, think about the fact that you are trying to get your hips to move forward in the water up to the point where your hand entry occurred. If you just pull your hand before you get your hip moving, you don't stand a chance. So how can you get your hip to move before you pull? How about rotation?

ROTATION

Coach X has started to see more and more "studies" appearing in swimming magazines telling swimmers not to rotate or at least not to rotate so much. Coach X disagrees. When Coach X does a swimming clinic he often does drills to get swimmers completely rotated on their side. This has drawn criticism from many coaches. There is however a very good reason Coach X asks swimmers to do this.

The reason is that most swimmers do not rotate *enough* during their swims. Instead they rely on their hand pulls to move forward. A proper rotation will engage what we call "the kinetic chain". This is a transfer of energy from your hip all the way through to your fingertips. The best example that Coach X can give you is to think of a baseball pitcher throwing a ball. Think about how he winds his hips and rotates his hip first, then his torso, and finally his arm. If a pitcher just used his arm, the ball probably wouldn't even get to home plate!

Coach X believes that swimmers need to learn how to use that rotation to drive their body forward when swimming. Of course what Coach X believes doesn't really matter. Facts matter; and these facts happen to be laws of physics. Converting that rotational energy into forward momentum will make you faster in part because it will drive your hips forward without the need to pull your arm as much. This is the secret to a good anchor. In fact Coach X will go so far as to say that many swimmers simply cannot anchor without rotation.

TIP: Rotation should drive your hips forward to the point of your hand entry, NOT your pull!

So why does Coach X ask swimmers to go all the way from side to side during swimming clinics? As mentioned above, most swimmers do not rotate enough during their races so Coach X wants to over emphasize the feeling. What Coach X learned over the years is that, in general, it is a good idea to over emphasize at slow speeds; as swimmers begin to go faster the rotation will naturally begin to become a little less. At sprint speeds there is still less, but it is now exactly the right amount. If you practice drills with the same rotation you would swim at race pace, then the rotation will often disappear completely when you swim the race all out. For this reason Coach X recommends that when you are doing drills, you should exaggerate how much you rotate at slower speeds.

This is why Coach X cringes when he sees popular swimming magazines printing things like "Don't rotate" or "don't over rotate" in their technique sections. It is statements like this that cause swimmers and coaches to overreact. Coach X thinks that what these publications really mean is that swimmers *should* rotate, but when you swim fast you wouldn't want to be going from side to side. To Coach X, and probably to you, this seems obvious. When magazines print things like this they do a lot to destroy technique and make swimmers slower. Coach X has seen this first hand at swimming clinics all over the world. Coaches that read things like "don't over rotate" tell their swimmer *not* to rotate, and that is the wrong message. So *Super Sprinters* – keep rotating!

TIP: Always exaggerate your rotation during practice! It ensures you will not under rotate during a race.

HOW TO PULL

What other secrets can Coach X share with you to make your anchors more effective? Here is one that you simply need to know, especially if you are one of those swimmers that does a lot of dry land training such as weight lifting. If you haven't yet read "Eric's Story" earlier in this book, you should go back and read that now. To refresh your memory, Eric was on a team where the head coach had the swimmers on an aggressive weight lifting program. The coach argued that swimming fast was nothing more than pushing more water. In a very simplistic way, that is at least 50% true. Leaving aside the whole notion of simply reducing drag to increase speed: if you are relying on your arm pull to make you fast, then you will not want to skip this section.

Over many years, Coach X has viewed underwater video of literally thousands of swimmers. There is one thing that is almost universally true – the more you rely on your arm pull, the worse your arm pull is. Most swimmers that work very hard to be able to put a lot of force on the water want nothing more than to jump in the pool and beat up the water. Guys are considerably more guilty of this than girls. And come on, it's a total guy thing to do; when you are strong you want to let the pool know it! I mean if you're taking hours each day to train your muscles, you're going to darn well use them.

> **POP QUIZ: Which of these arm pulls is correct:**
> 1) When your hand enters the water, immediately pull straight back as hard as you can.
>
> 2) When your hand enters the water, pause, then

pull straight back as hard as you can.

If you've been reading this book from start to finish you will already know the answer is neither number one nor number two. The real answer is number three; keep reading.

RACING DOWNHILL ON BIKES

When Coach X was little he used to love riding his bike down a really big hill near his house. Coach X had an awesome three speed bike. It had high, medium and low gears. Just before reaching the hill Coach X would get the bike into high gear and could get up to almost 40mph. Then he would hit the top of the hill and try to ride as fast as possible all the way down. But no matter how fast he would pedal, he simply couldn't get the bike to go any faster. No matter how much additional energy he put in, it wasn't enough to keep up with the momentum of the bike.

Sometimes when Coach X was at the bottom of the hill, and ready to go back up, he would forget to put the bike into low gear. As soon as he started to go uphill it became almost impossible to move forward. Coach X would need to stand up and exert a huge amount of energy just to move the bike a few inches. Often this was so difficult that Coach X would just fall off of his bike.

What can we learn about swimming from Coach X's bike story?

TRENT'S STORY

Not too long ago Coach X met a great high school swimmer named Trent. He was a tall, very strong, muscular swimmer and an awesome student who loved his high school chemistry class. One day in class the teacher was doing a lesson on metabolism and energy sources. Trent was paying very close attention because he often felt as though he did not have enough energy to drive a fast arm rate during his races. It was the peak of the high school season and he wanted to drop some serious time in his 100 yard front crawl.

Over the last week, as part of a class assignment Trent had to record what he ate and figure out his body's metabolic rate on an average day. He found this to be very cool! Trent figured he could use this information to determine just the right foods to eat before his next swimming meet.

On the day before his next big event, the chemistry teacher was talking to the class about the amount of energy stored in various types of foods. Trent was wondering what food would pack the most energy. His teacher then let loose the Holy Grail! "Triglycerides contain a triple bond and contain the most amount of energy," The teacher said. But where do you get triglycerides? The answer came shortly thereafter as the teacher then said, "The best source of triglycerides in your house is probably Carol's syrup, but you wouldn't want to drink that; it would taste awful!"

Trent got a smile on his face. He knew exactly where a bottle of Carol's syrup was in his mom's cabinets. He never knew what she used it for, but he was determined to get his arms moving as fast as possible at his next meet. The next day, Trent used the math he already did to find his metabolic rate. He calculated exactly how much syrup to drink and approximately when he needed to drink it in order to get the maximum energy for his race. Just for good measure he also put in two raw eggs and some white chocolate for taste. He downed his glass of "pure energy" that was calculated to peak during his 100 free.

At the warm-ups Trent was on fire! He was hopped up with more energy than a chipmunk in the spring. There was so much energy coursing through his body he could barely contain himself. Before the swimmers were allowed in the pool, Trent was jumping and running in place. His coach was impressed!

Then Trent jumped in the pool and took off like greased lightning. Nothing could stop him. For the first time in a very long time, Trent found that he was able to cycle his arms as fast as his mind could imagine. There was virtually no limit to his energy. Eventually the coach noticed this and told Trent to "save something for the race!"

When the race finally came, Trent was still bouncing all over the place and found it hard to stay still on the block. He barely managed to avoid a DQ from a false start! As the starter sounded, Trent made his entry into the water and everything felt absolutely amazing! By the third length, where Trent would normally feel very fatigued and tired, he still was bounding with energy. Trent's arms were spinning out of control. His stroke rate was well over 100 strokes per minute!

On the last length, Trent came sprinting into the wall. He was sure that he dropped at least seven seconds with his new cycle speed. To his surprise he did not. It turned out that Trent had dropped only about two seconds and it had nothing to do with his super-fast stroke rate. Rather it was entirely due to his kick! Because Trent had been kicking and cycling so fast, he very quickly reached a point where the force he was applying to the pull was not even close to his forward momentum. When this happens, regardless of how strong you are, your pull on the water does absolutely nothing!

While Trent was a strong kid, he reached the point where his body was moving too quickly for his arm pull to be effective at the higher cycle rate. The only thing that helped his time therefore was his kick.

TIP: To maintain speed during a race, it is considerably more important to maintain stroke length rather than stroke rate.

Without knowing it, when Coach X was riding his bike down big steep hills, he was experiencing some more very cool laws of physics. These same laws affect your body when swimming in the water. What you need to know is that once your body is moving, there is a limit to how much force you can put into your pull and still be effective. This is important to know. It means that no matter how much dry land weight lifting you do, at some point you are going to reach that limit where your bike (I mean body) is moving so fast that your pedaling (I mean pulling) doesn't have much affect anymore. Coach X certainly is not saying to stop lifting the weights, but rather keep in mind that you're not going to become a *Super Sprinter* by weight lifting alone. You need to recognize when your maximum force is outweighed by your forward momentum and glide. As your body slows down you will reach a point at which your pull force will again become effective. That is when you should begin your pull.

TIP: There is a limit to the effective force you can apply to the water. When your momentum exceeds your maximum force, you are wasting energy.

If this all is a little hard to follow, don't worry. Coach X is going to break it down in a way that makes sense. Rather than whip out the Force equation (nothing to do with small green guys in swamps), Coach X is going to give you an experiment so that this will all make sense:

CORDS OF SPEED

For this experiment you are going to need to put on your suit. This experiment does require the use of stretch cords which you can attach to the starting block. Coach X recommends the cords not be rated more than twenty-five pounds of force – we do want you to get to the other side of the pool!

Simply attach the cord around your waist and begin to swim front crawl. You will notice that it becomes harder and harder to make any forward progress, but you need to make it all the way to the other side. Feel free to grab onto the lane line and pull yourself across if necessary.

Once you are at the other side, hold onto the wall and make sure you have someone at the starting end of the pool to pull on the cord and take up all the slack for you. When you are ready have the person helping yell, "go!"

Try to swim as fast as you possibly can, applying as much force as possible to each arm pull. You will quickly realize that your body has so much forward momentum that your meager little arm pull simply cannot provide enough force on the water to keep up. No matter how hard you try to increase your stroke rate or pulling force, you are simply being pulled forward through the water by the cord. You are unable to provide enough power to continue to accelerate.

When you are moving very quickly in the water, it does not matter how strong you are. By applying force without accelerating, you are just wasting energy and warming the water for the other swimmers.

UNLICENSED PARTICLE ACCELERATORS

But wait, there's more you need to know! This is where the secret to a good anchor and good pull come in. To put the most force possible on the water, you need to do something very counter intuitive; especially if you are a strong, buff, guy. You should not just pull back as hard as you can. Instead you should start slow and then accelerate your hand as you go. It sounds crazy but if you simply push as hard and as fast as you can you will be causing the water to resist you at the square of your force. In addition you will cause the water to find the easiest way to get away from the force of your hand.

Think of an accelerated pull as sneaking up on the water. You go slowly at first and then just when the water thinks you are going to be nice, *Bam!* you go to full acceleration and the water is at your command. By accelerating your hand during the pull of any stroke you will become more efficient. That means that you will go faster using less energy, so when the person in the lane next to you is about to die, you will keep on going!

TIP: Always accelerate your hands through the pull for increased efficiency.

If you've ever wanted to play with cornstarch and water, then Coach X has a great experiment for you. Mixing these two components creates what is called a non-Newtonian fluid. Cool science names aside, here is an awesome experiment you can try in your kitchen. It will give you the idea of why accelerating is better than going all out immediately in your arm pull. Keep in mind that this is *not* what happens in water. Water does not become solid if you hit it suddenly, but this experiment is still really cool!

NON-NEWTONIAN FLUIDS

Grab a medium size bowl and a box of corn starch. For a really good effect, Coach X recommends using two cups of corn starch and two cups of water, but you can certainly do this experiment with less.

Mix the starch and water in the bowl using a spoon until it looks like all the starch is dissolved in the water. Now slowly stick the spoon into the mixture. Notice that it seems just like water.

But now, take the spoon and hit the surface of the mixture very hard and very quickly. Notice that the liquid resists the spoon!

BLOWING THE CURVE

A long time ago, Coach X was doing some experiments (Coach X is always doing experiments) and he discovered something very interesting and strange. It turns out that there are some swimmers, usually Olympic caliber swimmers, who blow away the curve for the rest of us. These swimmers are actually able to swim more than one body length per stroke cycle! How do they do that? Learning this little secret is truly important if you really want to become a *Super Sprinter*. So listen up, Coach X is about to let you in on some really cool inside information here.

It turns out that if you practice very hard at reducing your body drag, you can actually maintain forward motion during the recovery, or glide portion, of a stroke. In fact, if you are really good at it, you can maintain so much propulsion that by the time you start to slow down, your hips have already moved near your anchor spot. By the time you apply some additional propulsive force, your hips will actually have passed in front of your anchor! Wow – this is truly amazing to see because it will appear almost as if the swimmer isn't even trying but they will appear to be moving at a blazingly fast pace nonetheless. This is the state that every *Super Sprinter* must learn to achieve.

TIP: By reducing drag during the recovery, swimmers can move more than one body length per stroke cycle.

FUN WITH MATH

If you like math, and even if you don't, there is a fun little exercise that you can do to compute your optimal speed in any stroke. Simply measure from fingertip to fingertip, in inches, using a tape measure and write this down. Now divide 900 inches (25 yards) by your fingertip to fingertip length. That is half the number of strokes that it should take for you to get across the pool with a proper anchor at one stroke per second (60 strokes per minute).

There is a theoretical limit to how fast you can move your body. For most people, that turns out to be about one body length per second. So do the math. The answer you got above is the time, in seconds; it should take you to swim one length if everything were 100% perfect. Unfortunately, it's never perfect, so you can never actually reach that limit. Or can you?

ICE SKATES OR A TABAGON

If you are one of the lucky swimmers that live in a cold climate that gets snow each winter, then you will know all about ice skating and sledding. If you live in one of the warmer areas of the world, then you may not know about these things, but you are still lucky to live in such a nice warm place. Just about everyone probably knows what an ice skate looks like, but many of you may not know what a toboggan is. Simply put, a toboggan is a long wooden sled used for hurtling down hills at high rates of speed. Believe me, when you get those things nice and waxed up, it feels like you are flying at 100 miles per hour!

Why are we talking about winter recreational activities in a book on swimming? Well, it is because these are the two ways that most people swim front crawl. There are a lot of swimmers out there that look like toboggans when they swim. They tend to stay flat on their stomachs and they look straight ahead. Then there is another group of swimmers that rotate nearly all the way to their side on each and every stroke. For a brief time they look like an ice skate and you can almost imagine someone skating as they rotate from side to side because it reminds you of a skater shifting her weight from foot to foot.

Since there are two main ways of doing something, the question arises again – is one way better than the other? The answer isn't always yes, but in this case it definitely is!

Say you are in a group of kids up on top of a large hill. You just took out a new six person toboggan, you waxed it up and you are ready to have some serious fast fun. You are absolutely certain that your wooden machine is the fastest thing on the icy hill today.

Just as you are about to push off, a rival group shows up with their brand new sled. And guess what – this one is on skate blades. Which one do you think is going to win? If you said the sled on skates, you are right. The reason is that too much of the toboggan will touch the snow and ice. This causes friction which causes drag. The more drag on an object, the slower it will go.

Now imagine the same thing in the water. Well, okay, maybe not exactly the same thing. Coach X does not want you to put sleds into the pool – they might rust! But, imagine that your body is like those sleds. If you swim front crawl on your stomach, you are exposing a lot of the surface of your body to the water. That's going to make a lot of drag and make you slower. If you rotate to your side and turn your body into a skate, less of your body will be exposed to the water; right?

Wrong!

And this surprises a lot of people. In reality, you are still exposing nearly the same amount of your body to the water. The difference is actually in how much you are exposing to the SURFACE of the water.

> **POP QUIZ: What are the fastest sea faring vessels in the world?**

You might start thinking of a cutter, battle ship or maybe an air craft carrier. While air craft carriers can certainly move a lot of weight quickly, they are not that fast overall. Battle ships and cutters can go pretty fast too, but they are mere turtles compared to another type of vessel. You may be thinking of a speed boat. But guess what, you would still be wrong! In fact the fastest sea faring vessels don't spend much time on the surface at all. The fastest of all vessels are the submarines! This is because any vessel on top of the water has to deal with surface tensions, shear forces, waves, and several other nasty drag forces. The smaller the amount of a vessel that touches the surface, the faster the vessel can travel in the water.

By rotating your body onto the side you could be reducing the amount of surface contact by nearly ten times! That's a huge amount of drag reduction! And, drag reduction is what being a *Super Sprinter* is about!

TIP: Rotating during your stroke can significantly reduce surface drag!

NOW HOW MUCH WOULD YOU PAY?

In some ways Coach X feels like one of those late night television commercials. As if reducing your drag was not enough, there is another benefit of swimming on your side that you do not get when swimming on your stomach: Automatic buoyancy.

What is automatic buoyancy? The best way to think of this is in terms of balance. Remember that when most swimmers kick, they don't get 100% of the energy from that kick to move them forward. Instead a whole lot of it simply pushes their hips back to the surface to rebalance their bodies. However, as a *Super Sprinter* you have now learned how you can balance your body properly on the water and gain nearly all of that kick energy toward forward motion. The only problem is that sometimes balancing on the water takes a lot of thought because you need to compensate for parts of your body that are more or less buoyant than others. With automatic buoyancy you don't have to worry nearly as much.

TIP: Proper balance means that more of your kick will go to moving you forward, dramatically reducing your times!

How does automatic buoyancy work? It's really pretty simple. Imagine that you are at the beach with one of those really big multi-colored beach balls. If you push the ball down into the water, just under the surface, not deep, and then let it go, a really cool thing will happen. The ball will pop up out of the water a couple of feet! This happens because the water is constantly pushing on anything you put into it; be it a beach ball or be it your own body. The deeper you go in the water, the stronger that pushing force becomes. That is why when you dive into the deep end of the pool your ears might start to hurt.

So you might be wondering, why don't I shoot up out of the pool when I dive to the bottom of the deep end? If you had this question, it's not silly. In fact it's not silly at all! It's a very, very good question. The reason is that the water would very much like to shoot you up out the surface just like a whale taking a breath, but it can't. And why not? Because of the weight of all the water on top of you! But what if you never went completely under water? What if some part of your body was breaking the surface the whole time, then what? Then you would be pushed up by the water pretty hard. Unfortunately there are not many pool toys that happen to be twelve feet tall, but if there were, you can imagine how hard it would be to get that toy underwater!

How can we use this knowledge to become an even faster *Super Sprinter?* By now you have probably already guessed the answer. We do it by swimming on our sides. By turning your body sideways more of your body goes deeper into the water. The deeper your body reaches, the more force the water will use to push it up. The more force the water uses to push you up means less force your legs need for that purpose, and more force your legs can use to push you forward. The end result – a faster swimmer!

One very important quick note; Coach X mentioned it earlier, but it is important to say it again. The faster you go, the less far you will rotate from side to side. This is not to say that you will not rotate from side to side at race pace. The reason you should rotate less at race pace is that rotation takes time. The further you rotate from one side to the other, the more time it will take. When you start to get to a very fast speed, there comes a point where the benefit you get from the extra buoyancy is outweighed by the extra time and energy it takes to do that rotation.

TIP: The further you rotate, the longer it takes. At race speed you will naturally start to rotate less than when you practice.

When you practice each day at slow speed, you should still try to rotate as far as possible from side to side. As you go faster, you will naturally rotate less and normally there is nothing you have to consciously do. If you are one of the small number of swimmers that has trouble with rotation at high speed, have your coach take a look at you when you are swimming at race pace and they will be able to assess if you need more or less rotation.

GET BENT

One of the most overlooked areas for improvement is when we take our hands and arms out of the water. Far too many coaches and swimmers are only focused on what the hands and arms are doing while *in* the water. Coach X is simply amazed at the diversity of recoveries that he sees, and really scared by how many swimmers don't understand just how badly they are slowing down because of poor choices in their recovery.

WHAT GOES UP MUST COME DOWN

At some point everyone has probably heard the old saying that what goes up must come down. It's a fact of life and all too true. Most swimmers would think that this doesn't apply to them, but they would be very, very wrong. While Coach X loves science and math, he understands that some, very small portion, of you swimmers out there may not. So, Coach X will spare you the scientific details and give you a simple experiment you can do yourself.

CENTER OF GRAVITY

The next time you are doing a backstroke kick set, lift one of your arms up out of the water at about forty-five degrees. Do not kick any harder, and just watch what happens. Most of you already know what is going to happen – but try it anyway.

Repeat this experiment but this time lift your arm straight up out of the water. Hold it above your head and observe what happens. Finally, do the experiment again with both arms straight up out of the water. How much more of an impact did this have?

To really get a feel for it, go ahead and kick with one arm at your side and begin to slowly move the other arm straight up and back down again. Think about what is happening during each time you do a backstroke arm recovery. What can you learn from this experiment?

The laws of physics are pretty simple on this one. Anytime you move something out of the water, even a tiny little bit, it is going to push something else down into the water. That something else is you! That's not good. The problem is even worse when you lift something above your center of gravity. Unfortunately for us humans, our center of gravity in the water is near our lungs, and that just happens to be the same location where our arms are attached. This means that swimmers that bring their hands above their elbows are doing the equivalent of hoisting a five pound brick out of the water. In the water, weight that is close to the center of gravity has a very large and immediate effect, causing you to sink and lose your balance very quickly. The result is a much slower stroke.

The solution is to keep your arms very near the surface of the water. Ah ha! So that must mean that I should swing my arms around and keep them straight. As it turns out there are an increasing number of very fast National Level swimmers doing exactly that. However, Coach X is never one to get caught up in all the hoopla. Most of them are still wrong! There are a few reasons why recovering with a straight arm is not a good idea, but in truth there are also some good reasons to do it too. Let's talk about both, and then you can decide for yourself.

Here is a great example of how art and science merge in swimming. For 99.999% of us, a straight arm recovery is not the right answer. But guess what, if you fit the right profile and you meet that particular rule of thumbs, then it is entirely possible that a straight arm recovery will actually work better for you. Generally if you are a pretty buff guy, quite muscular, have trouble properly bending the arm and have the shoulder and arm strength to pull it off, then you should at least give straight arm recovers (and pulls for that matter) a try. If not, read on and learn some of the pros and cons.

TIP: Avoid moving anything too high above your center of gravity; keep your hands lower than your elbows!

JUST A PINCH

Over the years, Coach X has seen many swimmers from other teams come to him with some severe shoulder problems. Many of these swimmers ended up requiring surgery; some as young as thirteen! Believe me, surgery of any kind is not a fun matter. It's very serious and it's something to be avoided. The one thing all these swimmers had in common was a straight, upward, arm recovery in front crawl. The body is simply not designed for it – period. When you recover in this manner, it forces what is called a muscle impingement. In simple talk, it is squeezing your muscle and often pinching your nerve each and every time you recover with a straight arm. Over time, these impingements add up and lead to some very severe shoulder damage that will eventually require surgery. The problem is that many coaches and swimmers are unaware of this danger and do nothing to prevent their swimmers from recovering with a straight arm. If you are a swimmer that has started recovering with a straight arm in front crawl, for your own health, Coach X highly recommends stopping immediately; but, ultimately you will be your own judge.

If you are waving "Hi Mom!" on every recovery, there is more to worry about than muscle impingement. Remember from one of our experiments that anytime you put something above your center of gravity, it's going to cause problems. By moving your hand above your elbow during the recovery, you will lose balance on the water, sink and rapidly increase your drag. The net result is a much slower time in your race. *Super Sprinters* never wave to their parents while swimming during a race; save the hugs until you are out of the water.

TIP: Never lift your hand above your elbow during recovery in front crawl! Doing so can create muscle impingements and add drag to slow you down.

SOCKS, SHIRTS AND BROWNIES

With all of that bad news you may be wondering why anyone would ever want to swim with a straight arm. The main reason is that one swimmer sees another faster swimmer doing it and naturally thinks that must be why the other swimmer is going so fast. It is human nature to blame what is most noticeable for a result even if it is unlikely or even impossible to be the real cause. Just ask any baseball player about the rituals they "must" go through before a game to ensure a win. There's the lucky shirt, the socks that can't be washed for three weeks, eating a double chocolate brownie after each inning and on and on. All of these things had absolutely nothing to do with that player winning or losing, but it was readily observable at one time when a win did happen, so they assume incorrectly that it must have been the cause. The same is generally true in swimming. Not just in strokes, but especially in swimming apparel.

TIP: Recognize that just because something is observable, it may not be the cause! Avoid superstitions that don't actually improve your time.

STRAIGHTENING IT OUT

That being said, there are some interesting potential benefits to using a straight arm recovery and while Coach X really hopes that you choose not to use straight arms, he would be remiss if he didn't tell you the other side. So here it is. When Coach X asked swimmers why they used a straight arm recovery, here are some of the answers he got: a horizontal straight arm recovery (similar to one arm butterfly) will slightly increase your body rotation, it helps recover your arm more rapidly, and finally it allows you to enter further in front of your body to increase your stroke length. Let's take them one at a time and separate myth from fact.

It is true that when you extend an arm away from your body you tend to rotate toward that arm. However to properly engage your kinetic chain, the hip rotation should start about when your elbow is passing by your ear. By using a straight arm recovery, swimmers often throw their arms low and outside; like a one arm butterfly. This causes the hip to rotate before your body is in the optimal position. The result is less power in the pulling hand and less of your rotation gets turned into forward speed.

Some guys however have very large muscles and have very limited ability to bend the arm properly. If you are a buff college swimmer or high school swimmer that has this problem, then you may need to use a straight arm recovery. You will still have the muscle impingement problem to worry about if you lift your arm up. However, if you keep it low, then the sheer power of your arm pull may more than compensate for the loss of the kinetic chain. For this reason, very strong male swimmers may prefer a straight arm recovery *and* pull.

For the rest of us, the amount of rotation is extremely limited with a straight arm recovery. Remember that hip rotation helps to reduce drag and improve bouncy. These two factors make a huge difference in overall time and stroke efficiency. By reducing them with a straight arm recovery you are going to slow down. Coach X has seen no evidence (i.e., not a single study) that a straight arm recovery improves your speed.

Watching swimmers on video shows absolutely no speed increase in the recovery time. In fact, it shows that most swimmers using a straight arm recovery do not spend enough time gliding. This becomes a big problem in longer races like 200 meter front crawl events. As the swimmers reach exhaustion, they are unable to maintain proper distance per stroke and begin to fall behind in the last 50 meters of the race.

TIP: Avoid straight arm recovery in longer races! It tends to cause problems with maintaining distance per stroke when fatigued.

Next we will consider that a straight arm recovery will help you to get your arm in front of your head faster. To date, Coach X has been unable to find any scientific data to support this. If you swim this way, it may definitely *feel* faster because your hand will feel heavier when you swing it with a straight, outstretched, arm. But the feeling of acceleration doesn't mean that it actually *is* moving any more quickly. To prove this to yourself, do it both ways using a video camera. Time them both and you most likely will see very little or absolutely no difference in time.

Finally there is the notion that a straight arm recovery will help you to enter the water further in front of your head. In some regards Coach X can understand why swimmers would think this is possible. As you swing that hand around it is like throwing a tether ball on a string. You generate a lot of outward moving force. That force can actually pull you slightly in a given direction. As you throw your hand around and enter the water, you may get a slight stretch at the end which will let you enter the water slightly longer than a traditional entry. However, again there is nothing in the scientific studies to show that this is the case.

Even if there is *some* effect, it is almost certainly not going to give you the same reach as you could get with proper rotation. Since a straight arm recovery reduces rotation, this means that it also is shortening your reach. Plus, keep in mind, the same force that is getting the arm to stretch is also pulling on the shoulder joint in a way that can potentially injure the shoulder. Conclusion; the idea that straight arm recovery gives better reach or allows a faster entry are both myths.

Still not convinced that straight arm recovery is a bad idea for most swimmers? Here's another reason for you. Remember that it is more efficient to swim underwater than over water. The main reason for this is due to surface drag. By swinging the arm around the side, most swimmers create a slapping situation when entering the water. This results in increased surface drag.

SMOOTH AND FAST

It is actually much better to enter the water smoothly. Many swimmers will find a better approach is stabbing into the water and extending (reaching) your arm forward just before entering. In other words your arm should be almost straight, just a little bent, and almost fully extended as you spear in the water. Your fingertips should all enter at the same time and before any other part of your hand or arm. This helps to reduce surface drag and keeps the speed of an "in air" recovery.

KINETIC ENERGY

If you ever had the opportunity to watch a baseball game or pitch in little league, then the idea of a kinetic chain will be very easy for you. Baseball pitchers train in a way that makes Coach X often wonder: If they were to swim in their off season, might they actually have an advantage over other kids? You see baseball players learned a long time ago about a powerful tool called the kinetic chain of momentum, and unfortunately it is something that far too many swimmers have completely forgotten about.

When you watch a baseball player throw a ball, pay very close attention to what part of his body moves first. Your first instinct will of course be to think that his hand will be the first thing to move, but are you really sure?

Look a little closer. If you pay very close attention, you will realize that the person throwing the ball is actually leading just slightly with their hip. It becomes pretty obvious when you watch the pitcher throw the ball. He can get so wound up with his hips that he actually has to swing his leg around. But take a look at anyone throwing a ball a great distance and you will see the same thing.

In fact, it's not just baseball but other sports as well. Take golf. Any professional golfer would be no better than you or me if they did not know how to use their hips during the swing of the golf club. In football, the quarterback must rotate his hips to throw that long bomb downfield. There are of course countless other examples.

Why is it so important for athletes in these sports to rotate their hips before or during the throw? Because it creates what is called a kinetic chain of momentum. Wow – that just sounds cool! How does it work? Think of it like compressing a very powerful spring. When you release the spring, it expands rapidly and can be used to push something out in front of it. When you rotate your hip backward, it is like compressing a spring inside your body. By rotating your hip forward, you release that spring and all of the stored energy moves forward all the way down your body, out your hand and into the ball; or into your pull.

If you need another example, think of the "perpetual motion" toys you see in many stores in which there are about five balls, each hanging from a string. When you pull up on the ball on the far right and drop it, the ball falls down and smacks into all the other balls causing the ball on the left to pop up into the air. The ball on the left then falls back to hit the others, causing the right ball to popup into the air. The cycle continues until all the energy is used up. What is happening here is a transfer of kinetic energy between the balls. This is the exact same type of energy transfer that happens in your body when you invoke the kinetic chain of momentum.

What it means to swimming is this: By rotating your hips *before* or *during* your arm pull, you will achieve *significantly* more power in your stroke. How significant? In many swimmers we are talking about several seconds worth of time difference! Imagine your favorite baseball pitcher buried in dirt up to his arm pits. How far do you think he could throw the ball like that? Not too far at all. So here is a fun little experiment that you can do to demonstrate the immense amount of force that you personally may be wasting by not invoking your kinetic chain of momentum.

TIP: Rotating your hips slightly before or during the arm pull generates significantly more power.

KINETIC CHAIN

On the pool deck take a soft squishy pool toy. In a safe area

88

without people around go ahead and throw that toy as far as you possibly can.

Mark your foot position and mark the position where the toy landed. Now have a friend grab you around the torso and prevent you from rotating at all. Again attempt to throw the toy as far as you possibly can (this time without rotating). Mark the position where the toy has landed this time. Now go out and measure the difference.

Coach X likes to do this experiment with swimmers at clinics. He has seen many swimmers that can throw the toy clear across a 50 meter pool the first time and barely make it past a single lane the second way. Once you see how much extra power you can generate using your kinetic chain, you will hopefully never forget to rotate your hips before you start to move your arm again.

Unfortunately, when you watch most swimmers with an underwater camera you very quickly learn that they are not using their kinetic chain of momentum. Typically they will enter the water with their arm and once the arm is fully extended, then they will rotate their hips; and in so doing completely waste all of that stored energy. Again, this is generally due to the fact that few coaches and fewer swimmers are even aware of the kinetic chain of momentum or of its importance. To be a *Super Sprinter*, you must learn to engage your kinetic chain of momentum.

WHAT ARE YOU LOOKING AT?

Before we begin the next section, Coach X wants you to do another experiment. You will need a friend for this one. If you are able to video tape yourself swimming, that's even better. All you need to do is swim a 200 IM and have your friend watch you as you swim. Your friend's goal is to count how many times you breathe during each length. Remember to count your own breaths for each length!

After the 200 IM, get out and compare notes! See if your friend was able to correctly count your breaths. If she was, then you have a problem. Here is why:

ONE THING YOU HARDLEY EVER SEE

Summer is a great time for Coach X to watch the new swimmers in their lesson programs. It helps to remind him of just how much a swimmer really needs to evolve their stroke to become a *Super Sprinter*. When a swimmer first gets into the pool they are going pretty much on pure instinct. Since we spend most of our time walking around on two legs on land, the water can be an awkward place for new swimmers. One thing you hardly ever see is a brand new swimmer enter the water and keep their head perfectly still while they swim. Instead you see them looking all over the place. It is even rarer to find a new swimmer that does not look straight ahead of them as they attempt to move through the water.

When people walk on the land, they generally look forward to prevent themselves from walking into walls, poles and other people. If you were to look down at the ground while walking around it is very likely that you would run into someone or something. How many times has your mom or dad told you to "look where you are going!" With all of that day to day reinforcement it is easy to understand how even young swimmers will immediately look straight ahead in the water.

TIP: Keep your head looking directly down at the bottom for better balance and buoyancy.

The problem with looking forward when swimming is that it really messes up your balance. Because human beings are designed for life on land, our center of gravity changes in some strange ways when we are in water. Once in a pool, humans become very poorly designed see-saws. Imagine a see-saw on land where someone has moved the middle balancing point much further to one end than the other. What that means is when there is a very small change to the end closest to the balance point, there is a huge change on the other end. It also means that you need to push really hard on that short end of the see-saw to make the big end move up and down.

TIP: Each 1" you lift your head drops your hips by about 3"! If you are tall, the effect is even greater.

Now that really should scare a lot of people. It means that if you are looking straight ahead of you, your legs are going to naturally want to fall straight down to the bottom of the pool. And think about it, when you are getting ready to leave the pool your legs are underneath you so that you can step up on the ladder, and where are your eyes looking? Straight forward or even up into the air. That's certainly not the position that you want to be in when trying to swim.

Coach X has seen speed improvements of around 7% on average by having swimmers simply change their head position! WOW! It really does make a huge difference in the amount of drag on your body, and on the amount of kick energy going toward forward momentum versus pushing your hips back to the surface. Therefore the impact is twofold. By simply changing the angle of your head you benefit by reduced body drag and increased energy efficiency.

POPULAR MAGAZINES

There have been popular magazines targeted to age group swimmers that suggest that it is not a good idea to look straight down when swimming. Instead the magazine suggested that swimmers should "not look straight down, but swim with a head position that allows for a natural alignment and a straight spine." Now Coach X is very aware that there is a curve in the neck, but really? Did these guys never see an X-ray? Did they not pay attention when they walk on land?

If you put any thought into the advice from this particular magazine you will quickly realize that this advice doesn't make any sense as it is impossible to have a "natural alignment" and a "straight spine" *unless* you are looking straight down. This particular magazine told swimmers to look slightly forward. A very small amount of head tilt won't make too much of a difference in your time, but it will make some difference. Coach X thinks the only reason the magazine said not to swim looking straight down is because so many swimmers look forward including Olympic swimmers. But like Coach X says over and over; Olympians also have stroke flaws. Coach X would much rather put faith in science and physics than in anything else, and the physics are clear. You need to look down; straight down.

LEG LAYOUT

When you swim you want your legs to be as close to parallel with the surface as possible. That means that you want them to be in a straight line with the surface and not at an angle. If your legs are not in a straight line with the surface, then some part of your kick will be used in pushing your body up to the surface without your knowledge. For those of you who are having trouble staying above water, even though you are kicking very hard, this is why. Even if you are a very fast swimmer, winning nearly every race, you may not realize just how much faster you could be by simply looking straight down at the bottom of the pool!

TIP: Keep your legs mostly straight with just a slight bend and near the surface to reduce drag.

BALANCING ON A RAZOR

To be a *Super Sprinter* you will need to do more than just swim on your side and look down, you will also need near perfect balance. The truth is that looking down while on your side may require a little effort on your part while practicing your drills. Some swimmers are not sure when they have reached the perfect body position that will maximize both kicking and arm power. Fortunately, it is pretty easy to tell when you have it right. You will look something like a razor blade cutting through the surface of the water. Remember that you want to minimize how much of your body is exposed to the surface, but you still want some part of your body to break the surface. To do this, use your top arm and hip as a guide. If your top arm is dry from shoulder to hand, and if your hips are breaking the surface, then you've got the right position.

While doing this test you may find that your head is sinking too far under water. If your hips are breaking the surface, your hand is dry, but your shoulder and head are wet, then chances are that you are pressing too hard on your shoulder or face. Back off with the pressure just a little and you should find the correct position easily. Many male swimmers will suffer from this condition until they learn to back off the pressure just a little.

TIP: If your hips are breaking the surface but your shoulder is wet, release some pressure from your face and shoulder to level out.

If you are experiencing the opposite problem you will have a dry shoulder, but your hand and hips will be wet or even under water. To fix this problem just press down slightly in your arm pit and press your face down toward the bottom. Again, you should see the results almost immediately. The thing to remember here is to use small inputs. Very small changes in pressure can have very big effects on your balance. Until you can continuously swim with proper balance, Coach X recommends taking things very slowly. Give yourself a chance to pay attention to your body's built in indicators. Once you feel that you have the balance right, then slowly start to add back speed until you are once again back at race pace.

TIP: If your hips are wet and your shoulder is dry, increase pressure on your neck and face until you are level in the water.

WHY HOBBITS ARE POOR SWIMMERS

Now for one of Coach X's favorite *Super Sprinter* tricks. Here is something that any swimmer can do right now, today. It does not involve any extra energy. It does not involve extra yardage or extra training of any kind. You won't even need any special equipment. Yet, despite all of that, this one little trick could easily make you up to 7% faster in your stroke! What is Coach X talking about? He is talking about staying long in the water.

Most swimmers are familiar with the drill called catch-up freestyle. Staying long is a lot like that. It means that you want to trick the water into thinking that you are much taller than you really are by keeping one arm extended in front of your head as much as possible. Another term used to describe this is front quadrant swimming.

TIP: Staying in a long body position can improve your time by 7% using absolutely no additional energy!

One day Coach X was reading some forum posts on a swimming website when he came across a post titled "Does size really matter?" Nearly every one that responded to the question indicated that in fact size really did not matter all that much. Perhaps they did not want to hurt anyone's feelings, or perhaps those people that replied simply did not know the truth.

Whatever the case, they were dead wrong.

In swimming – Size Does Matter. It is no accident that most of today's world record holders are all over 6' tall. In the future as more and more world records are shattered we will continue to see taller and taller swimmers. Coach X would love to see someone 7' tall swim in the Olympics and shatter every world record in existence. The problem of course is that in our country anyone over 7' is not going to be swimming; they will be making millions as a basketball player in the NBA!

Why does size matter so much? It goes all the way back to an observation made by ship builders centuries ago. They discovered that the longer they made a boat, the faster it would travel through the water. For example, a boat that is 100' long x 40' wide travels slower than a boat 200' long x 20' wide even though overall their area is identical. The reason is all about Science! And as you know, Coach X just loves Science!

In simple terms it works like this: The longer an object, the less drag it will have. As you know, in swimming the less drag you have on your body, the faster you will travel. Therefore, longer swimmers go faster not because of extra power but because of less drag. In fact they may not even necessarily have a longer distance per stroke. They can go faster simply because being tall means they don't slow down as much during the recovery. If you are paying attention you will have just discovered something very interesting. This means that taller swimmers can go faster than shorter swimmers without using any extra energy at all! Wouldn't it be great if a shorter swimmer could do that?

TIP: Longer, skinnier objects have less drag and move faster through the water.

Good news – shorter swimmers can get the same advantages as tall swimmers by simply staying long in the water when they swim. What this means to you the *Super Sprinter* is pretty easy. When doing front crawl, keep one arm in front of your head, reaching out as far forward toward the other side as possible until your other hand begins to enter the water. Do not pull your arm yet! Wait until your rotation makes your stroking hand pass your extended hand and then pull back. It's not catch-up stroke because your hands will never actually touch. Instead your hands should pass by each other out in front of your head. Continue to do this on every stroke and you will have magically added as much as 20% to your body length. Without using any extra muscle power or energy you will immediately begin to see significant time drops!

TIP: Short swimmers can get the same drag reduction as a taller swimmer simply by staying long in the water.

Coach X tells many swimmers to do a simple pre-race ritual. When you stand up on the blocks, clap your hands over your head. As you do so look to the left and to the right. You can easily see that with your arms over your head you are by far the tallest swimmer in the race. That means that all things being equal, *you* are going to win! Since most swimmers do not know about the advantage of staying long, they tend to immediately pull their arm backward as soon as it hits the water. The result is they are swimming short. If you practice swimming long, you will have a major competitive advantage over your fellow swimmers. As mentioned above, this simple technique requires absolutely no additional energy from you, yet it could increase your speed by as much as 7%! That is why this remains one of Coach X's favorite *Super Sprinter* techniques.

TIP: Clap your hands high over your head on the block to show yourself that if you stay long, you are actually taller than your competitors!

S PULLS AND CORK SCREWS

Earlier in the book we talked about the myth of the 'S' pull when swimming front crawl. To refresh your memory, this was due to an attempt to imitate a very famous Olympic swimmer. The swimmer's name was Mark Spitz. Coach X remembers a conference where the famous 'S' pull was discussed. According to the discussion, the 'S' pull allegedly came about from something like this:

Mark's coach at the time decided to use some state of the art computer analysis to figure out what made Mark such an incredible athlete. To do this he attached tiny lights all over Mark's body and put him in a pool where he could be filmed. The idea was that Mark's movements would be tracked by watching how the lights moved in the water. According to some tales the next thing that happened was very interesting.

The story suggests that at a press conference one day, Mark appeared with his coach and other trainers. Someone from the press asked Mark what was different about the way he swam that made him so fast? Mark replied that he didn't really know, he just reached in and pulled straight back. This same story says that at that moment Mark's trainer leaned forward and put an arm out in front of Mark and said "No, No, No, That's not it at all!" He then went on to explain that using the fancy lights they were able to determine that Mark was actually making an 'S' with his hand as he swam through the water. Meaning that he would scull outward, then back inward, then back out again. Shortly thereafter many books were written on the 'S' pull. College and High school coaches across the nation began making their swimmers use this miraculous new method for super speed. Oddly though, it never seemed to really work very well. For many this became a mystery.

As it turns out, it was no mystery at all. The puzzle was solved years later when someone thought of viewing the light pattern not only in two dimensions, but in three dimensions. Taking Mark's words to heart it was realized that to an outside observer you could get the exact same effect if you entered your arm straight in front and pulled straight back *while rotating your body*! Since in Mark's time body rotation was not at all common, it was not even considered as part of the equation. In fact Mark was absolutely correct about how he was swimming. There never was a true 'S' pull in the sense that the high school coaches were promoting – and which by the way many coaches still insist on teaching.

In fact Mark was pulling while rotating his body causing a spiral or corkscrew effect. The simplest way to see this is to take an old toilet paper tube and unravel it. You can see the spiral groove going through the tube, but if you unravel the tube you will see that it is really a straight line.

TIP: Don't make an 'S' with your hand! Rotate and pull straight back.

THINGS TO AVOID

Coach X would like to take a moment to congratulate all of the readers that have gone out and started using some of the techniques and tricks that we have already talked about, and tell you about a few things that you will need to pay attention to while learning.

Most swimmers do not have access to an underwater camera, but if you do – use it! A great product you should consider is the *GoPro!* Hero series camera. They are fairly cheap and are not only full HD cameras, they are completely water proof! If you don't want to buy a camera, then it is a good idea for you to put on a pair of goggles, go underwater and hold your breath for a while. Take a look at the other swimmers in the pool when they take a breath during front crawl. You will notice that just about every one of them will use their hand to push down on the water as they lift their head for the breath. The reason that most swimmers do this is because they are not properly balanced. It is also because most swimmers do not breathe correctly in the front crawl. Rather than turning their head to the side with their body rotation, many swimmers tend to lift their heads up. As we already learned, anytime you lift your head you force your hips to sink. There are only two ways to save yourself in that situation. One is by kicking harder and the other is by pushing down with your hand.

TIP: Never push down with your hand when breathing.

There are a couple of problems with using your hand to push down during a breath. First, it is never a good idea to have anything sticking out of the imaginary tunnel created by your body as it goes through the water. Anytime something goes outside your bodyline it is going to create drag. Drag is bad; it makes you slow.

The second reason the hand push is bad regards what it does to your balance. If you watch the hand push with an underwater camera and freeze the frame you will always see that a small peak forms between the torso and the arm. You will also see that at this moment there is usually a slight angle to the line that goes from the hips to the toes and that the hips are slightly underwater. This bend in your body adds drag, but it also creates a pocket full of water that you must now pull along with your body through the water. I don't know if you ever tried lifting three gallons of water, but it is not light. Towing all that extra weight, even for the short time of a single breath, can really slow you down.

Finally the hand push slows you down by making you swim shorter than necessary. As we learned above, your body's drag is reduced when your arm is fully extended out in front of your head and in the water. When you do a hand push during a breath you cease being long and consequently increased the drag forces on your body. All in all that is a lot of drag, so it is best to avoid doing a hand push during a breath. Instead practice, every day, keeping your arm extended in front of your head as you roll to breath.

TIP: Connect your breathing to your rotation! Do not lift your head to breathe.

It will take some time to get used to doing this. Bad habits die hard. But through lots of practice and hard work, it will eventually come naturally to you. It is a good idea to have someone watch you underwater or video tape using an underwater camera about once a week to make certain that you have mastered this new *Super Sprinter* skill.

BREATHING

Is there any swimmer out there that doesn't already know that breathing slows you down? If not, Coach X is here to let you know that it is true. Are you a science geek like Coach X? If so, you will want to know *why* breathing can slow your times. As with most problems, there are a couple of things at play here.

First, breathing is the main thing that affects your buoyancy. Remember that humans are built funny. In water, how much you fill your lungs will determine how much and how quickly you float. When you are swimming like a true *Super Sprinter* you are focusing on balancing in a straight, level, line. Inflating your lungs can cause your body to pivot, making your legs and suit sink slightly. This means that you have to actively think about controlling your balance as you inhale. In the middle of a race, no swimmer is going to be thinking about that; it's just not going to happen. The problem is that these factors all increase drag on the swimmer and slow you down.

Second, breathing affects your starts and turns. Remember that you will be going your fastest during your start and during your push offs from the wall. The longer you are able to stay underwater while maintaining a high rate of speed, the faster your overall time will be. There are several swimmers out there that tend to take a breath right before a turn. Now Coach X knows that if you are one of them, your coach has almost certainly told you to stop doing that. But even if you do not take a breath right before your turn, many swimmers still take a deep breath on the start or take a huge breath only a few strokes away from the wall. The thinking is that you are going to be underwater for a while and you are going to need all the air that you can get.

Too many swimmers take way too much air with them off the walls and on the starts. This means that they are affecting their buoyancy! By taking a deep breath a swimmer inflates his lungs which will make him more buoyant. The increase in buoyancy means that it will be much harder to stay underwater. The swimmer will end up using more energy just to stay underwater and even with that extra force; he will still surface rapidly and lose out on all the advantages of a speedy underwater start or push-off. The result is slower times. Coach X has seen several young swimmers drop one to two seconds in a 100 yard swim simply by working on the amount of air they carry on a start or turn.

The *Super Sprinter* must learn to exhale some air or to only take a short breath during a start and while doing push-offs. The slight reduction in air in your lungs will allow you to stay underwater longer and get out much further into the lane. Remember, you are fastest underwater. Don't waste that valuable distance floating to the surface too quickly.

TIP: Take only as much air as you absolutely need on a start or turn! Exhale as you go to stay underwater longer.

LESS IS MORE

Time for an experiment! Go suit up and hop in the pool. We are going to work on streamline push-offs and prove that less air is more distance. As always, a video camera pointed at your lane would be best, but if you don't have one, try to take something along that you can rest on the lane line to mark how far you go on each push-off. Clothes pins or hair clips work really well! First go ahead and do your best regular push-off. Do not kick! When any part of your body breaks the surface, stand up and mark that position. Now perform the push-off the exact same way except this time exhale about half of your air before you go. Again wait for any part of your body to break the surface then stand and mark the spot.

One of two things is likely to happen in this experiment. One is that you will stand up and be completely amazed at how much further out in the lane you are standing. The second is that you find that you never break the surface and that you have run out of air. If that is the case, then you should try to take a little more air, or try not pushing off quite so deep (remember – waist deep is a good measurement).

Now repeat the above experiment with kicking. After a few attempts, you should quickly find exactly how much air you need to reach your maximum distance. When practicing always try to pay attention to how much air you are taking with you on the starts and in your turns. If you practice at maximizing your distance by breathing during your practice, it will carry over into your race and you will soon find that you have become a *Super Sprinter*! Remember, you want to stay under water only as long as you remain fast. Once you begin to slow you should be at the surface and ready to race.

CROSSING UNDER

One of the most common and major problems swimmers have is crossing an arm under their bodies while swimming. Even good swimmers can often be seen committing this sin when they take a breath. Be warned *Super Sprinter,* this is very slow! Coach X has a great solution to this problem. From years of observing thousands of swimmers, he has tracked down the source of this common problem. Coach X hopes that you are sitting down when you read this because it may shock you.

Never, and I mean never, streamline while doing a front crawl kick set! Seriously. That is the source of the cross under. Think about it, every practice your coach probably yells at you to streamline when you kick and what is that teaching you? It is teaching you that your hand belongs in front of your head when you are swimming front crawl. Well guess what? It doesn't!

By having swimmers kick in a streamline, coaches are setting their swimmers up for disaster! It creates muscle habit that navigates that hand right back to that exact same position when you are in a race. The result is that you pull your arm across your body when you rotate. Bad, bad, bad!

The solution is super simple. Whenever you do any front crawl kick set, make sure your arms are shoulder width apart and kick like you are superman. This generally isn't a problem if you are kicking with a board. However, Coach X is aware of some boards that are *designed* to force the swimmer to streamline. If you have one, through it away!

TIP: Never kick in a stream line when doing a front crawl kick set! This will set you up for crossing under your body during a race and will significantly slow you down.

BREAKING OUT

Since we are talking about starts and push-offs from the wall, this seems like a great time to bring up the topic of front crawl break-outs. Coach X thinks this is important because he has heard coaches give some very "interesting" advice when it comes to breakouts. So let's put some science on it. If you think about it, what we really want to do is maintain as much speed as possible off every wall. We've already learned from other parts of this book that doing a body dolphin is much more powerful and efficient than a flutter kick. We've also learned that the optimal depth off the wall is right at the crisscross point of the target painted on the wall.

Putting these two ideas together, we can quickly figure out that the best approach is going to be a fast, powerful, body dolphin off each wall and off the start, about two feet under the surface, with just as much air as needed. The question then is, when to take your first stroke? Coach X has heard many different opinions on this.

One train of thought is to wait until you completely break the surface before starting your first arm pull. The idea being that breaking your body line will increase drag. That is true, however if the timing is done correctly, it's actually a very good idea to start your first arm stroke before surfacing.

The trick is to start the arm stroke at the exact moment where you transition your kick from body dolphin to flutter kick. To do this right, you will want to push off the wall (or start) with a fast body dolphin. At the moment you begin to slow, switch to a flutter kick and start your arm pull. If you do it right, you should be at the surface as you are starting the second arm in motion. This maneuver will allow you to keep maximum speed off the start and off every wall. Coach X has personally witnessed this technique allow swimmers to completely destroy the competition off the wall.

TIP: When doing a front crawl break out, start the pull when you transition your kick from dolphin to flutter.

FRONT CRAWL TIP SUMMARY

GENERAL

TIP: Train to improve both your physical stroke and reduce drag during your recovery to double your time drops!

TIP: Never use weight training alone to improve your speed. The amount of weight needed is the square of the amount of force you need to apply on the water!

BALANCE

TIP: Keep your head looking directly down at the bottom for better balance and buoyancy.

TIP: Each 1" you lift your head drops your hips by about 3"! If you are tall, the effect is even greater.

TIP: If your hips are breaking the surface but your shoulder is wet, release some pressure from your face and shoulder to level out.

TIP: If your hips are wet and your shoulder is dry, increase pressure on your neck and face until you are level in the water.

ROTATION

TIP: Rotation should drive your hips forward to the point of your hand entry, NOT your pull!

TIP: Always exaggerate your rotation during practice! It ensures you will not under rotate during a race.

TIP: Rotating during your stroke can significantly reduce surface drag!

TIP: The further you rotate, the longer it takes. At race speed you will naturally start to rotate less than when you practice.

TIP: Rotating your hips slightly before or during the arm pull generates significantly more power.

DRAG / RESISTANCE

TIP: Your speed in a race is never constant. Learning to be slippery during a recovery can improve your overall time as much as three months of hard training!

TIP: Reducing drag during recovery costs no energy and will drop your times over 10%!

TIP: Body length matters in swimming! The longer your arms (not your body), the faster you will swim!

TIP: By reducing drag during the recovery, swimmers can move more than one body length per stroke cycle.

TIP: Short swimmers can get the same drag reduction as a taller swimmer simply by staying long in the water.

TIP: Longer, skinnier objects have less drag and move faster through the water.

PULL

TIP: Do not squeeze your fingers firmly together when doing a pull. A very small amount of space is actually good as it widens the hand and creates more surface area during the pull.

TIP: There is a limit to the effective force you can apply to the water. When your momentum exceeds your maximum force, you are wasting energy.

TIP: Always accelerate your hands through the pull for increased efficiency.

TIP: Never lift your hand above your elbow during recovery in front crawl! Doing so can create muscle impingements and add drag to slow you down.

TIP: Don't make an 'S' with your hand! Rotate and pull straight back.

TIP: When doing a front crawl break out, start the pull when you transition your kick from dolphin to flutter.

ANCHORS

TIP: Anchor properly by not pulling on your hand until your hips pass the point of hand entry.

TIP: When anchoring properly, your speed should equal one full body length per stroke cycle.

KICK

TIP: Proper balance means that more of your kick will go to moving you forward, dramatically reducing your times!

TIP: Keep your legs mostly straight with just a slight bend and near the surface to reduce drag.

TIP: Never kick in a stream line when doing a front crawl kick set! This will set you up for crossing under your body during a race and will significantly slow you down.

SPEED

TIP: To maintain speed during a race, it is considerably more important to maintain stroke length rather than stroke rate.

TIP: Avoid moving anything too high above your center of gravity; keep your hands lower than your elbows!

TIP: Recognize that just because something is observable, it may not be the cause! Avoid superstitions that don't actually improve your time.

TIP: Staying in a long body position can improve your time by 7% using absolutely no additional energy!

TIP: Avoid straight arm recovery in longer races! It tends to cause problems with maintaining distance per stroke when fatigued.

TIP: Clap your hands high over your head on the block to show yourself that if you stay long, you are actually taller than your competitors!

BREATHING

TIP: Never push down with your hand when breathing.

TIP: Connect your breathing to your rotation! Do not lift your head to breathe.

TIP: Take only as much air as you absolutely need on a start or turn! Exhale as you go to stay underwater longer.

BACKSTROKE

"A dream doesn't become reality through magic; it takes sweat, determination and hard work."
Colin Powell

BACKSTROKE

It will probably surprise a lot of people to learn that backstroke is not the stroke that most swimmers say they want to swim. At least it surprised Coach X. I mean how much easier can you get? You don't have to worry about your breathing, you just kick your legs and wave your arms and you generally move. Of course those of you that have already become *Super Sprinters* in backstroke already know that this isn't true. For one thing, the name of the stroke isn't even right! Coach X loves giving this question at swimming clinics all across the world. Let's see how you do:

> **POP QUIZ: Backstroke is swum:**
>
> A) On your stomach
> B) On your side
> C) On your back

This is what we call a ridiculously easy test, but unfortunately about 99% of the swimmers that take this test fail! What did you pick? If you picked A, you're just right out! If you picked C, you didn't do much better. The correct answer, believe it or not is B – On your side. See, I told you that they didn't name the stroke correctly.

WHAT'S IN A NAME?

Many swimmers seem to think that because backstroke is called "back" stroke that it is supposed to be done on your back. Nothing could be further from the truth!

Swimming on your back causes all kinds of problems, not to mention that it's slow. For one thing, it causes you to veer off course quite a bit. That's because you are making your arms bend in some very unnatural ways. If you happen to also be stiff arming your pull, you are in for a world of hurt – literally. You are very likely creating impingements in your shoulders that are likely to lead to some sever shoulder pain and possibly much worse. You also end up going rather slow because you have a lot more surface area in the water which increases your drag. Drag is bad. Drag makes you slow. Your one job above any other as a swimmer should be, at all times, to reduce drag! Then you have the wonderful laws of physics. Those laws of physics are something that Coach X likes very much, because if you understand them you can actually go faster using less energy than you did before!

TIP: Do not swim backstroke flat on your back. Rotate to a maximum of forty-five degrees on each side.

When you swim any stroke one thing that you really want to focus on is balance. You want your body to remain fairly level in the water when you swim backstroke. You might think that is easy to do when you are on your back, but it isn't. Every little bit you lift your head out of the water forces your hips to drop down, when your hips sink, you increase drag. And as we have seen; drag is bad! By swimming on your side you allow your body to get a little deeper into the water while still maintaining a portion of your body breaking the surface. This actually helps make you become more buoyant. The water will push you to the surface more easily and without as much effort from you. The less time you need to spend worrying about good body balance, the more time you can focus on going fast! So for all of these reasons swimming on your back is just a bad idea.

PANCAKES AND STEAM ROLLERS

It just so happens that two of Coach X's favorite movies both involve people being run over by a steam roller. I don't know why, but there's just something terribly funny about seeing someone flattened by a slow moving machine that takes half an hour to move a very short distance. If you have ever seen "Austin Powers International Man of Mystery" or "A fish called Wanda", you will know what I mean. If you haven't seen those movies, just imagine how flat you would be if you got run over by a steam roller. You might say that you'd be as flat as a pancake. That's exactly how Coach X describes the proper head position in backstroke.

If you go to an age group swimming meet and watch the backstroke events you are very likely to see several of the swimmers with their heads held very high out of the water. Remember that for every one degree you lift your head up out of the water, your hips are going to sink about three degrees! In order to stop sinking you will need to kick harder. The problem here is that by kicking harder you are not making yourself move forward any faster! You are only kicking your hips back to the surface.

This means that you are literally wasting your energy. All the kick energy that goes to pushing you up to the surface could be going to push you forward. To solve this problem and get back all that energy, all you need to do is pretend you are a pancake on the water. Your head should be completely flat on the surface. If water washes over your face now and then, that is a good thing! Your entire cap should be under water. In fact the cap line just above your eyebrows is a very good measure of whether or not you have a proper head position. The water line should meet your cap line. If it does not, you need to push your head down into the water more. Note: Coach X said push down, *not* tilt back!

TIP: Flatten your head by pushing down, not by tilting!

106

FLAT HEAD

It's time to put your suit on and jump in the pool for another experiment! In this experiment you will get to see for yourself what Coach X is talking about. The experiment is really easy. You are going to start by pushing off on your back at the surface of the water with your arms and hands at your side.

If your coach is watching, they will probably be screaming at you to streamline, but ignore them for now. All Coach X wants you to do is kick very, very slowly. Start with your head as flat as possible on the surface. As you kick, slowly begin to lift your head up out of the water. Continue to slowly lift it until you are actually looking back at your feet. Then do the opposite. Slowly lower your head back to the surface and even start to tilt it under the water. What did you observe during this experiment? What happened to your hips as your head came up?

A "HEAD" OF THE REST

Since we are not water animals (fish), we sometimes have a hard time understanding some generally simple concepts when it comes to water. In order to properly balance your body you want to have a flat head. This means that you are going to have to apply some pressure to your head to get it down in the water. Think of pressing a beach ball down into the water. When you do this near the surface and let go, the ball will shoot up out of the water. This is the same type of thing that you want to do with your head. By pressing it down into the water you are allowing the water to push up on your whole body. When you do this right, the water will push up your hips and your suit will even come out of the water just slightly.

TIP: Your suit should just barely break the surface at all times when swimming backstroke!

But the key is to do it right. You do not want to tilt your head nor to bend your neck when pressing your head down into the water. Keep your neck neutral. Just pretend that your best friend is magically hovering about one foot above you in the water and you are having a conversation.

When you speak to your friend on land (assuming he or she is the same height as you), you do not look down or up. If you did your friend would think you are weird. Instead you look straight at them, eye to eye. This is the same head and neck position that you should have when you swim backstroke. Keep your neck straight and your head neutral then press your head down into the water until the water line comes to your cap line.

TIP: Push your head into the water until the waterline matches your cap line on your forehead.

Once you get this position, try pressing down on your shoulder blades. Push both your head and shoulders down into the water until you feel your suit break the surface. This is how much pressure you should be swimming with routinely while doing backstroke. If you do this, darn close to 100% of that kick energy will move you forward and not be wasted keeping your hips at the surface.

TIP: When balanced in backstroke, nearly 100% of your kick energy will push your body forward!

You know you've got it right when your suit breaks the surface just a little bit while you swim and kick. If it's not breaking, you need to put more pressure on your head or shoulders until it does. Remember to not arch your back or to tilt your head. It's all about pressure on the water. Stay relaxed but also flat. When you can get your suit to slightly break the water the entire time, you will immediately start to see a drop in your times.

TIP: Never arch your back! Push straight down between your shoulder blades to bring your suit and legs to the surface.

ROLL, ROLL, ROLL YOUR BOAT

In the introduction to this chapter we briefly described why swimming on your back is not a great idea. Now it's time to examine why and to figure out how rotation can improve your backstroke times and help to make you a *Super Sprinter*.

COACH X GOES TO WASHINGTON

One day a few years back, Coach X was walking through the Smithsonian Museum in Washington D.C.; it's awesome! Being a major science and history buff, museums are Coach X's favorite place in the world (it used to be the library, but today we have the internet). The Smithsonian is one of the world's greatest museums and the Smithsonian Natural Science Museum is one of the best in the world, so Coach X was in heaven while touring the amazing exhibits. Unlike many people, when Coach X goes to a museum he actual reads everything and often goes out of his way to find a museum curator to ask questions. In fact he once spotted an error regarding salmon migration patterns while touring a museum in Canada which he brought to their attention for correction, but I digress.

On the day Coach X toured the Smithsonian Natural Science Museum he came across an exhibit of fish over time. The exhibit showed, on the right end, very ancient fish and as the exhibit moved to the left the fish evolved to modern. One thing immediately caught Coach X's attention. The fish on the far right all swam flat in the water. That is to say that instead of the tail swaying back and forth, it moved up and down. As the fish evolved, this motion disappeared until in modern fish it was gone almost completely. Coach X did not think this was a coincidence so he found a museum curator to speak with.

The exhibit curator was extremely excited to speak to someone. Coach X guessed that he didn't get many questions. In any case, the scientist told Coach X that no one had ever noticed this in the exhibit before; or at least they hadn't mentioned it to him. According to the Smithsonian scientist, this exhibit was the perfect example of how we can use nature to learn about our physical world.

For these fish the laws of physics were something unfathomable. To them it wasn't merely a matter of being able to come in first, second, or third. It wasn't about being heat winner or getting a medal. It was quite literally life and death. Over millions of years, these fish were optimizing the way they swim to make the best use of physics so that they could have baby fish and avoid being eaten.

A FISH EATS FISH WORLD

We can learn a lot from this exhibit. Like humans swimming backstroke, fish did start by swimming flat, but because this added extra drag and due to fluid dynamic forces, and other laws of nature, those fish were slow. The same is true for a swimmer on their back or stomach. Millions of years ago, a fish was born with a mutation or "defect" that allowed it to move its tail and swim sideways. It was so much faster that it was able to evade predators and thus it was better able to have baby fish. This change was so advantageous that fish without this ability soon went extinct as they were eaten by the faster fish. So the question is: Do you want to swim on your back and be eaten by others, or do you want to swim on your side and be the one eating the competition for lunch?

No story could have been clearer: Swim flat and die, swim on your side and live. The same is true for humans in the water (although not in life and death terms). Those same forces that evolved water animals to switch from flat swimmers to side swimmers affect you too! Swim flat and lose, swim on your side and win.

TIP: Swim backstroke on your side to reduce drag and move faster through the water!

ROLLY POLLY BOBBERS

Now when Coach X says, "Swim on your side", does he really mean completely on your side? The answer is no. You will often see drills that will have you completely on your side, but those are drills. When you swim, how far you rotate from side to side will depend a lot on your speed in the water. The problem that Coach X often sees in the water isn't too much rotation, but rather a complete lack of it.

How many times have you watched an age group swimming meet and observed several swimmers bobbing up and down as they go down the lane doing backstroke? Coach X sees this happen way too often and wonders to himself how any coach could see a swimmer doing that and not work on rotation the very next practice. This problem can be amplified if the swimmer is both swimming flat *and* has their head up out of the water rather than flat on the surface. To be clear, when your body rotates, your head does not. Your head should remain still during your entire race (except of course during the turn).

TIP: Avoid bobbing by keeping your ears under the water and rotating your body with a still head position.

To fix this bobbing problem, the swimmer needs to rotate their body as they swim. How far should you rotate? Here is a simple rule of thumb: Roll just until the side of your suit breaks the surface on each side of your body. There is an easy way for guys to measure this. On most briefs there is a seam in each side of the suit. Simply pretend that the seam is your mouth. That seam needs to clear the surface of the water so that it can breathe. This will put your body in roughly a forty-five degree angle to the water on each side. Remember that it is critical that you balance properly while rotating. This means that some part of your suit should be breaking the surface at all times as you roll from one dry top hip to the other. In other words, at some point as you go from side to side you will be on your back and in that moment, your suit must still be breaking the surface.

TIP: Shift your pressure during rotation! Some part of your suit should break the surface even while rotating from side to side.

CASTLES, BOATS AND CANNONS

Coach X always makes sure to watch the backstroke events when he goes to swimming meets. For many years he has been astounded by the lack of swimmers that know how to swim backstroke correctly. There are the obvious problems like pulling with a straight arm, swimming on the back instead of the side and swimming with the head up. But there are some more subtle problems as well. While they may be small, these problems are what can really make the difference between a mediocre swimmer and a *Super Sprinter*.

READY – JOUST!

A long time ago, brave knights would have tournaments of honor and skill. One event involved using long metal poles called lances. The knights would charge toward each other on their horses while extending their lance in an attempt to knock the opposing knight off his horse. If you ever get a chance to see a joust you should go. But even if you don't live near a Renaissance Faire, you can still watch a young knight joust against his opponent.

The next time you go to a swim meet, be sure to watch the backstroke events. Take a look at the first heat of swimmers and then take a look at the last heat of swimmers. One thing that you are likely to notice is that the first heat (the slower swimmers) are pulling their arms like a windmill and cycling through the water so fast their arms look like something on a Saturday morning cartoon!

In the later heats, you are likely to notice that the swimmers are keeping their arms on the surface. That is, after the recovery, when the hand hits the water, it stays there! It does not pull until the other arm is almost directly overhead. It almost looks as though they are using their arm as a lance and using it to joust with the water itself. This practice is called staying long. Delaying the pull will keep your body longer in the water and thus will reduce drag. Guess what? – It Works!

What the swimmers in the later heat have figured out is a really cool way to trick the water. They have found a way to make the water think that they are actually much taller than they really are. As we, the longer and more narrow a vessel is in the water, the less drag it will have. Simply sticking your arm out in front of you in the water can be more effective in dropping your times than a full body technical suit! Remember, the trick is to *keep* your arm in front of you as long as possible. A good rule of thumb is to extend your arm until you see your recovering arm directly above your eyes, then roll your hips and pull with the extended arm.

TIP: Never immediately pull your hand when it enters the water! Always keep your arm fully extended in the water in front of you as long as possible to reduce body drag!

WALK THE PLANK

Another common problem occurs when swimmers try to rotate. It used to be a popular dance craze, but it has no business in swimming. It is called the twist, and as you might expect, it's slow! When you rotate you want to engage your entire body. Again remember that your head does not move. Pretend that your body is one long solid plank of lumber. Yes, you are a 2x4. If you imagine your body as a tree trunk then you can see all parts must roll at the same time. Avoid rolling just the top or just the legs, or worse, the top and legs at different times and different directions! Remember: everything rolls together.

TIP: Avoid twisting at the hips! Connect your body along the spine to reduce drag.

They say timing is everything. The big question is: When should the swimmer start the rotation? For now Coach X has this advice: Wait! Way too many swimmers favor a fast cycle rate over a long stroke when swimming backstroke and it is not a good idea. Because of this, many swimmers start rotating *way* too late.

Many coaches believe that if a swimmer waits until the recovering hand is overhead, before initiating the pull, their stoke rate will be too slow. Nothing could be further from the truth. But, you need to condition yourself to make it work well. Most swimmers fall into a trap when they begin to practice backstroke drills for body length. Far too often they are told to "hold" their arm extended in the water until they see the recovering hand over their head. While this is correct timing, the wording immediately creates a bad situation. It implies that they should be waiting. Too many swimmers translate this as "go slow!"

Instead, you should maintain your normal stroke rate during these drills. Try to keep at least sixty strokes per minute (or one per second). A tempo trainer can really help here. Using the metronome of a tempo trainer forces you to keep a fixed stroke rate while still teaching you to stay long in the water. The simple act of keeping your arm extended in the water out in front of your head can reduce your drag by huge amounts! For no extra energy you will suddenly be swimming significantly faster.

If you get the timing right you will see an abrupt and absolute increase in speed. This is because when the timing is correct, you will be turning that rotational energy into lateral (forward moving) energy. In other words, your rotation will actually make you move forward in the water! The really amazing thing is that you may actually feel like you are going slower because you will be using less energy!

TIP: When doing backstroke elongation drills, use a tempo trainer to maintain a high stroke rate.

HULA HANDS AND THE MACARANA

While we are on the topic of common mistakes, let's take a look at a few common problems with the pull. Coach X wishes he could say this next problem is limited to young or new swimmers, but it's not. The problem isn't actually a pull problem; it's really a recovery problem. Many swimmers will stretch their arms so far across their body that they actually have their left hand entering on their right side. I am not joking here people! Coach X has actually seen this several times!

When this occurs it does become a pull problem because the swimmer has to hyper extend their arm just to pull the water. It's a great way to get joint problems in the future. All of this can be easily avoided with a couple of precautions. First, as a *Super Sprinter* it is your job to be mindful while swimming. As it turns out, this is particularly hard to do in backstroke. Normally a swimmer ties an observation to the breath. It is easy to remember to ask yourself if you did something correctly every time you lift your head to breathe. In backstroke, you never lift your head, so many swimmers find it hard to stay mindful of their stroke.

Instead, there is a better solution. Never, ever, kick in a streamline when kicking backstroke! Yes, coaches, you heard me! Not only does this train your swimmers to lift their heads into a bad head position, it establishes a horrible muscle habit of bringing the hands to the center of the head, and that is *not* where they belong! When kicking a backstroke set in practice it is far, far better to do it slightly on your side with one hand on your hip and the other fully extended out in front of your head. You can use the extended arm like a pillow and rest your head on it. Plus, you don't need to worry about hitting the wall, or anybody else, with your head because your arm will protect you.

TIP: Never do a backstroke kick set in a streamline! It will create a muscle habit that will cause you to cross over on arm recovery.

There is another common problem with arm entries and pulls. Many swimmers know that it is important to rotate during the backstroke. Most of those same swimmers have coaches that instruct them to enter the water pinky first out in front of the shoulder. Coach X is sure that these coaches mean well, but again, this is *not* a good idea! Remember, the swimmer should be starting the hip rotation just as the recovering arm is directly overhead. If the swimmer is entering directly in-line with the shoulders, the hip rotation will actually cause the hand to enter over the head! Instead of targeting an entry in-line with the shoulder, *Super Sprinters* should target entering slightly wider than shoulder width. When the rotation is timed correctly this will perfectly align the arm in a straight line with the direction of movement. The result, pure speed and smooth strokes!

TIP: Enter your hand slightly wider than shoulder width! If your rotation timing is correct, this will properly align your hand entry for a smooth and fast stroke.

SPATULAS

Hand entry in backstroke can be a subject of great debate. Coach X likes to throw out the anecdotes and just look at the science. Lately, Coach X has observed a new trend in backstroke swimmers that seems especially popular with women. The idea is to have a perfectly straight arm recovering through the air with the hand bent outward at ninety degrees. It looks like a giant spatula. Coach X has done some research and believes he has even tracked down the source of this phenomenon. It is an article in a popular magazine that suggests this very method to age group swimmers, but with one slight difference. The article suggests that the swimmer should enter pinky first, then immediately extend the fingers to point at the side of the pool and initiate the pull.

If you have read this entire book so far, you will immediately see two problems with this advice. First is one that we already covered: You never want to pull your arm immediately because it would make you swim short and add drag. The result is that you would swim slower, not to mention that it would reduce your stroke length in a longer race and again make you slower. But there is another reason this is just plain bad advice. Anytime you have any part of your body sticking out to the side it is adding drag. This is easy enough to imagine without the need to actually do an experiment. If you were to use a hand paddle and point your finger tips to the far end of the lane versus point your finger tips to the side of the pool, you are going to notice an immediate difference! Coach X begs all those Super Sprinters out there to ignore this fad and ignore this advice. Keep your fingers pointed to the end of the pool until you are ready to begin your pull, *then* you can turn your hand into a spatula!

TIP: Do not enter the water with your fingers pointing to the side of the pool! This creates extra drag and will slow you down.

PENGUINS AND ELBOWS

Here is one thing that Coach X hopes he can get rid of. While Coach X likes penguins and thinks they are cute, he does not enjoy seeing swimmers do backstroke pulls with straight penguin arms! Too many swimmers in age group meets are still doing their underwater pulls with completely stiff arms and this needs to stop. It feels fast to most swimmers because it requires them to put a lot of pressure on the water. They figure that as long as it feels like they are pushing water, it must be making them move quickly. Well, no, no it does not.

Straight arm pulls in backstroke are just bad news! For one thing, if you are the type of backstroke swimmer that looks like a tennis ball bouncing between the lane lines, Coach X will bet that you are doing at least one straight arm recovery. This is because a straight arm recovery will actually direct the water to the side, not down the lane. As a result, your body will move to the opposite side of the lane. This doesn't do much to get you where you want to go!

TIP: Straight arm pulls in backstroke will cause you to bounce from lane line to lane line. Make sure you bend your elbow!

Most swimmers know to bend their arms in backstroke but they really don't appreciate why it is so important. Here is a really nice, quick experiment to show why.

LEVERAGE

Stand on the deck and hold one arm straight out in front of you, palm down toward the ground. Don't bend your arm or twist your body! Have a friend use only their pinky to push your hand up. Don't resist yet.

Have your friend count to three, and then your friend should try to push your hand up with their pinky while you try to push down your arm. Next, repeat the experiment. This time bend your elbow and keep your elbow above your hand. While you're at it try twisting your body slightly so that you are standing at an angle to your friend. When doing this version of the experiment, Coach X recommends that your friend use both hands to try to resist you.

What you should have learned is that when your arm is straight you have nearly no strength at all. It's fairly easy for your friend to push your arm up with just a pinky even when you try as hard as you can to press down. There is a lot to learn from this simple experiment. It means that when your arm is bent and your elbow is high you have a lot of power, when your arm is straight you have almost none.

A bent elbow in a backstroke pull significantly increases your leverage on the water! In addition, it directs the water directly behind you. The result is that you move forward in a nice straight line. No more smashing into lane lines!

TIP: Bend your elbow during the backstroke pull to significantly increase the force you can apply to the water!

ARM WRESTLING

One last point about the underwater pull for backstroke: It is very important that you do not lead with your elbow. Now that sounds a bit strange because, in truth when you do the pull correctly your elbow will be in front of your hand for a while. What Coach X means is at a very specific point in the stroke, you need to make sure your hand comes over and in front of your elbow. Picture that point where reach back, grab the water, and drop the elbow. Got it? Good, at that very moment when you have a ninety degree bend in your elbow, that is the moment that you want to arm wrestle with the water. Press your palm forward and bring the hand out in front of the elbow. Many swimmers get to that moment and continue to drive forward with just the elbow. This results in no power in the stroke. It is simply sliding the elbow forward through the water and going almost nowhere for the effort.

KIN-E-SEE-O-WHAT-ICS?

Lastly, Coach X wants to give you just a little advice about your kick. Most of you already know that you should body dolphin under the water as close to the fifteen meter mark as possible. You also know that you should have a nice long flutter kick. You already have heard: don't separate your legs too much, have a slightly bent knee, kick near the surface. So Coach X will assume that you are already doing all of that stuff. If not, start!

There are a few more things that you should think about though if you really want to be a *Super Sprinter*. The first is a bit of kinesiology. Simply put, that is the study of how the body moves. One of the things you probably never think about is how you look when walking on land. If you pay attention you will see that we move our opposite arm and leg forward at the same time. For example, if you step forward with your left foot, you will swing your right arm. This natural balance happens all the time without giving it any thought.

In the water however, things sometimes don't work quite as well. Your coach may have told you to do a six beat kick, meaning six kicks per stroke. When you are on land you certainly don't take six steps for every one arm movement, that would just feel too weird. So what Coach X often sees on slow motion video is a swimmer who is trying to do a six beat kick and is entering her right hand into the water at the same time as her right foot enters the water.

Some of you must be thinking, "Okay, so what!?" Well, no matter how you look at it, this is a problem. If the swimmer is only doing this once in a while, she will through off her entire balance and consequently her entire stoke timing. As you can imagine, that will result in much slower times. If the swimmer is doing this for every stroke, the problem only gets worse. By the way, if your coach ever tells you to do a three, five or seven beat kick, look at them very strangely because they are setting you up to fail. If the kick beat is odd, you will always mess up your foot/hand entry on every other stroke! When doing a six or eight beat kick, take the time to record your swims and make sure that you are entering the opposite hand and foot into the water. This practice also is true for front crawl swims or any time you are using a flutter kick.

Since we are on the subject of the kick, there is one more *Super Sprinter* trick that Coach X is going to share with you. This is definitely advanced stuff and it isn't for everyone. But there is a trick you can do in both your front crawl and backstroke to super charge your kick. When you get this trick right and imprinted into your neurology (that's your brain), you will drop some serious time. Probably enough to start shattering not just team records, but state records as well!

JESSICA'S STORY

At one of Coach X clinics, he met a young girl named Jessica. At only seven, she was the younger sister of the fastest swimmer on the team. Everyone paid a lot of attention to Jessica's older sister because she was very popular and she was a fantastic swimmer as well as a really nice person. But that was going to change! On the first day of a clinic Coach X always does under water video so that everyone can see their improvements on the last day.

As this was a front crawl / backstroke clinic, Coach X had each swimmer do a 50 yard swim across the pool doing their fastest front crawl down, backstroke back; with their best technique. Usually this is very close to race pace, but just a little slower to focus on technique. When it came time for Jessica to do her swim, Coach X saw something that he had only ever seen once before in another very young and very fast swimmer named Max.

Jessica ripped up the lane! She was not just fast, she was insanely fast! As she flew down the lane her Coach came up to Coach X and explained how Jessica had been crushing the team records for her age group. He wasn't quite sure what it was that she did that made her so much faster than the other kids in her group. From looking through the underwater camera, Coach X could see immediately what she was doing, and it was amazing!

This tiny little girl had told her coach that she didn't really like to swim front crawl or backstroke. As it turned out, she much preferred to swim butterfly. Coach X spoke to Jessica and her parents shortly after the initial video session to find out her history. It turned out that Jessica had only recently joined the swim team and had been to only two meets. Before that she was taking private lessons at the local pool. Why would such an amazingly fast swimmer need lessons?

Jessica used to play in her back yard pool all the time. Her parents noticed that she could move across very quickly and they decided put her on a swim team. But they knew that Jessica didn't know all of the strokes. When she went for her first lesson the instructor wanted to see what Jessica could do. The little girl jumped in and did body dolphin to the other side.

Not bothering to really see if she knew any other strokes, the instructor just assumed that Jessica already had lessons and just needed to finish off her butterfly. The instructor taught Jessica to properly use her arms and to breathe correctly then told the parents that she was ready for the swim team.

This brings us back to the clinic. It turns out that Jessica never learned to do front crawl or backstroke! When she joined the swim team, she started doing front crawl and backstroke arms with a body dolphin. The coach eventually got her to do the flutter kick in both strokes, or so he thought! Unbeknownst to him, whenever Jessica had the chance, she would not only do flutter kick, but would simultaneously do body dolphin as she rotated from side to side. She was actually rotating on both her short axis and her long axis at the same time! The result was simply amazing! Her stroke was so much faster using this kick that she simply destroyed all the other swimmers at every meet.

Coach X recently checked back in with Jessica and it turns out that she is still a super-fast swimmer. In fact, she has broken every record that her older sister ever set. She is doing this not by hundredths of a second, but by several seconds. Oh, and one more thing Coach X forgot to mention; Jessica's older sister is a National level swimmer! Meaning that in a few years we are very likely to see Jessica tearing up the pool at the Olympic Games.

TIP: When kicking in backstroke or front crawl, attempt to flutter kick while simultaneously doing body dolphin to significantly improve your times!

BACKSTROKE TIP SUMMARY

All Front Crawl Tips also apply to Backstroke (see FRONT CRAWL TIP SUMMARY)

BALANCE

TIP: When balanced in backstroke, nearly 100% of your kick energy will push your body forward!

TIP: Never arch your back! Push straight down between your shoulder blades to bring your suit and legs to the surface.

TIP: Avoid bobbing by keeping your ears under the water and rotating your body with a still head position.

ROTATION

TIP: Do not swim backstroke flat on your back. Rotate to a maximum of forty-five degrees on each side.

TIP: Swim backstroke on your side to reduce drag and move faster through the water!

TIP: Shift your pressure during rotation! Some part of your suit should break the surface even while rotating from side to side.

TIP: Avoid twisting at the hips! Connect your body along the spine to reduce drag.

DRAG / RESISTANCE

TIP: Flatten your head by pushing down, not by tilting!

TIP: Your suit should just barely break the surface at all times when swimming backstroke!

TIP: Push your head into the water until the waterline matches your cap line on your forehead.

PULL

TIP: Never immediately pull your hand when it enters the water! Always keep your arm fully extended in the water in front of you as long as possible to reduce body drag!

TIP: When doing backstroke elongation drills, use a tempo trainer to maintain a high stroke rate.

TIP: Enter your hand slightly wider than shoulder width! If your rotation timing is correct, this will properly align your hand entry for a smooth and fast stroke.

TIP: Do not enter the water with your fingers pointing to the side of the pool! This creates extra drag and will slow you down.

TIP: Straight arm pulls in backstroke will cause you to bounce from lane line to lane line. Make sure you bend your elbow!

TIP: Bend your elbow during the backstroke pull to significantly increase the force you can apply to the water!

TIP: When your elbow reaches a ninety degree bend in your pull, arm wrestle the water by getting the palm up and over the elbow for extreme pull power!

KICK

TIP: Never do a backstroke kick set in a streamline! It will create a muscle habit that will cause you to cross over on arm recovery.

TIP: Always enter the opposite hand and foot into the water during a six beat kick!

TIP: When kicking in backstroke or front crawl, attempt to flutter kick while simultaneously doing body dolphin to significantly improve your times!

BREASTSTROKE

"Don't be afraid to give up the good to go for the great."

John D. Rockefeller

BREASTSTROKE

Now this is one of the strokes for which there is a lot of controversy. For some people this is the simplest of all the strokes. From day one they jump in the pool and off they go, just like they were meant to be frogs or something. For most others this will be the hardest of all the strokes to master. This is particularly true because this stroke is so unlike any of the others. I mean think about it… in what other stroke do you kick like a frog? In what other stroke do you shoot your hands forward?

Because the arm and leg movements are so different from any other stroke, breaststroke is probably the most difficult of all the strokes to get really well. Then there are simply so many aspects to the stroke that it is hard to really know if you are doing it well. Is it better to bring your chest high up out of the water and then use the force to press forward? Is it better to recover your hands under water or over water? How wide or narrow should the kick be? Should the hips break the surface? Is it better to breath every stroke or only when necessary?

While there are a lot of questions to answer about this stroke before you can become a *Super Sprinter,* don't worry. We will answer all of these questions and maybe even a few others.

WHEN ONCE I HEARD THE LEARNED ASTRONOMER

Many years back, Coach X was sitting in a conference hosted by one of the top coach trainers in the United States. He worked for one of the various coaching associations and in his seminar he was to teach the best and most proper way of doing breaststroke. He told the audience that the "correct" timing in breaststroke was Kick, Pull glide.

Well, because Coach X always needs to know for sure, he decided to setup a simple little experiment, and you can all try this at home too. The thing about this experiment is that, while any swimmer can do it, it will work best with new swimmers who have never swum the stroke. Why is this? Because some swimmers have had certain timing drilled into them from the time they were four years old, and trying to change that timing to anything else is likely to feel awkward at first. With new swimmers that have not yet setup a timing system for their stroke, they can change the timing at will and not suffer from any habit memory.

PUSH PULL KICK

Ok, so here is what to do. Simply have a coach or a friend time you for a 100 breast. First do your breaststroke so that you start in a stream line position, then do a breaststroke kick, then immediately do a breaststroke pull and go back to a streamline. Record the time. Now do another 100 breast. This time again start in a streamline position. First begin by doing a pull, then a kick, then a glide; record that time. Finally, start in a streamline position, and begin with a fast "push". In other words, don't worry so much about pulling your arms back, instead focus on getting your arms back to that streamline position as quickly as possible, then glide for a second. Try saying, "I love breaststroke" in your head, then while still in the streamline, kick a breast kick and again glide for a second. Get a time for the entire 100 swim.

When you have tried all of these various ways (feel free to add a few of your own). Look at the times to see which of these methods produced the fastest time. If you really want a good comparison, have your coach or friend also count how many arm pulls or pushes you do with each 100.

After you do the experiment you will likely find that the method which was offered to all the coaches at the conference from the world expert is in fact the slowest and also takes the most number of arm strokes. The second method is generally a little bit faster but uses about the same number of strokes and the third method results not only in increased speed but also in fewer strokes – the best of both worlds!

TIP: Swim breaststroke using the mantra: Push – Glide, Kick – Glide

PROVING IS BELIEVING

This lesson is one that is echoed over and over in this manual. Never believe anything that you are told by a coach or an expert or even by this book! You must prove for yourself that what they say is true. Too often a so called expert will get the stage and try to convince us all that their way is the best way based on nothing but anecdotes or based on a single Olympic swimmer's quirks. Don't fall for it! The one thing that makes the *Super Sprinter* a truly great swimmer is that they validate things for themselves. Always remember that there is no better coach for you than you.

After doing the above experiment some of you may get different results than what I suggested the outcome ought to be. That's OK. Remember that everyone is a little bit different and there may well be something about you that is different enough that one of the other methods may be what works best. On the other hand if you have been swimming one of the other methods for a long time, you probably owe it to yourself to try the new timing for a while to get out of those old habits and then see if you don't get a marked improvement.

TIP: Always know this: You are your own best coach! Validate everything you are told.

BALANCING ACT

Throughout the book, Coach X has tried to emphasize the need to be balanced on the water. Believe it or not, you still need to stay balanced even when doing strokes like breaststroke or butterfly. Some swimmers may be questioning Coach X's sanity right about now. How can you possibly stay balanced in a stroke where you are going up and down all the time? Coach X will tell you the answer in just a minute, but first he wants to let you know that balance isn't just important in breaststroke, it is absolutely critical. In fact, balance in breaststroke is possibly more important than any other stroke.

Unlike front crawl and backstroke where you are swimming from side to side, in breaststroke you are flat on your stomach; huge drag. Even in butterfly, if you mess up your balance, you at least have a somewhat powerful kick to help move you through the water. Not so much in breaststroke. In breast, if your balance is off, you're not moving.

There are three main factors in a properly balanced breaststroke. Fortunately most swimmers don't suffer from problems in all three, but nearly everyone has issues with at least one. If you want to be a *Super Sprinter* then you will need to learn to balance without issues in any of these three main areas. Don't worry; it's actually pretty easy once you know what's going on.

TIP: Proper balance is critical in breaststroke! Stay level during each stroke when gliding.

DEEP SEA DIVING

The first thing Coach X wants you to know about breaststroke is that you are not a harbor seal! Watching many young swimmers learn breaststroke, and even watching some heats at age group swimming meets you can see kids that have forgotten about being human. When they do breaststroke, these kids apparently think they are a harbor seal. They dive nearly halfway to the bottom of the pool on each stroke cycle.

To get an idea of why this is a really bad idea, think back to our experiment with the beach ball. When we pushed a ball all the way down to the bottom of the pool and then released it, the ball took a very long time to surface. When it did, there was almost no energy left to push the ball out of the water. Swimmers that dive deep in the water during breaststroke are facing the same problem. Remember that the rules state that some part of your head must break the surface on every stroke, even if you don't breathe. That means that if you dive down, you've got to get back up to the surface. The rhythm of the stroke doesn't really give you time to just float back to the surface. That means that you must actively force yourself back to the surface. Therefore, you are using energy to push yourself under water and using energy again to force yourself back up. It's a much better idea to just stay near the surface in the first place.

TIP: Stay very shallow in breaststroke to avoid forcing your body to the surface on every stroke.

124

SEA SLINKY

This experiment will show you very quickly why staying on the surface is so important for breaststroke and butterfly. To make the point we are going to exaggerate things just a bit. You will need to put on your suit for this one. Coach X will wait.

Okay, now that you have your suit on, head out to the pool and have someone time you doing a nice slow, relaxed, 25 breaststroke. Try to really take the time to focus on your technique when you do this.

Next, start at the wall. Have your friend or coach time you for another 24 breaststroke. Do your regular breaststroke as fast as you can with the following change: Once you take your first breath, dive as far down as you can without touching the bottom. Surface for your arm pull and breath and dive down again.

The motion you are making is that of a giant slinky. Remember to do the second 25 as fast as you possibly can without touching the bottom. When you are done compare the two times. Coach X is going to guess that even though you went slowly on the first 25 and all out on the second 25, your first time will be much faster.

When you go up and down in the water, it is like making a link in a slinky. It might seem like no big deal, until you stretch the slinky straight. When you do, you will find out that you actually didn't swim a 25 at all, with all the up and down motion you may have actually swam more than 50 meters!

TIP: Diving too deep in breast actually increases the distance you have to swim and will kill your time. Favor a very small amplitude (up and down motion) when doing breaststroke!

Fortunately the deep sea diving exercise is usually only seen in very young swimmers and they quickly outgrow the problem. Then comes the next level of balance in breaststroke, and this really is the step that makes or breaks the *Super Sprinter*. Eventually you will learn that it is a bad idea to dive half way to the bottom of the pool, but it is not a bad idea to get under the wave turbulence at the surface of the water!

A really good swimmer will learn that with each arm push, they should dive just slightly under the surface. Going about a foot or so deep and holding is just about right. This depth is sufficient to begin reducing drag from the turbulence at the surface of the pool. Being underwater also means you have no surface drag, and reducing the drag means that you will move faster through the water. You should hold this position as you glide in a streamline until you naturally begin to rise in the water. Coach X tells swimmers to say, "I love breaststroke" in their head as they glide to give enough time to get out in front of the wake.

TIP: Get under the wake! Your hips should pass underneath the small wake you create in front of your body when you dive underwater.

Here is where the balancing act comes in. When doing the glide, your body should stay level. The longer you can hold a flat and level body position during the underwater glide, the faster you will go. To prove this to yourself you can either do an actual experiment or you can do this quick thought experiment: If you hold a kickboard level underwater it's pretty easy to move it forward. If you start to tilt that board at an angle, it gets increasingly difficult to move it in a straight line going forward. That's because when the board is tilted you are adding drag. Now imagine a kickboard the size of your entire body! That's exactly what happens when you force yourself to the surface for your next stroke. You are effectively coming to an almost a dead stop in the water!

TIP: Balance level during the glide. Shooting out of the water at an angle adds significant drag.

The *Super Sprinter* will know that the best thing to do is to surface naturally from the air in the lungs and will press down on their chest while underwater to ensure that their body is flat during the glide phase of the stroke. They will also optimize how far they go underwater versus how long they glide to ensure that they are not losing speed by staying underwater too long because they dove too deeply for the glide.

TIP: Optimize how far you travel under water during the glide! You should start the next stroke or kick before you start to slow down.

WHAT ARE YOU LOOKING AT!?

Lastly, there is one key element of balance that Coach X sees violated way too many times. Even some of the best breaststroke sprinters out there fall victim to this problem way too often. It is what we call "whack-a-mole" syndrome, and people, it is a horrible disease to catch! It doesn't matter what heat of breaststroke races you watch, eventually you are bound to see someone lift up their head and begin looking around. Sometimes they are looking for the competition, sometimes for the finish; sometimes they appear to simply be checking the weather.

No matter what the reason, it's *never* a good idea! In earlier chapters such as those on front crawl and backstroke we learned that lifting your head even one degree out of the water will cause your hips to sink as much as five times that amount. In a stroke that already has more drag than any other, the last thing you want to do is add more. When you lift your head out of the water, even to breathe, you are forcing your hips down toward the bottom of the pool. It's like slamming on a break, and it is really, really, *really* slow.

It is so slow in fact, that Coach X has a recommendation for you. This may sound crazy, but Coach X ensures you, it works very well. Did you know that it is perfectly legal to breathe every three strokes in breaststroke? Most swimmers have absolutely no idea that this is true. Many coaches simply are not aware or never really thought of the implications of this important rule. The fact is that only some part of your head must break the surface on each stroke cycle. Therefore it is far more efficient to simply keep your head down, allowing just the back to break the surface for at least three stroke cycles. This helps to maintain proper balance, keeps your hips high and greatly reduces drag. From this technique alone, Coach X has seen regular breaststroke swimmers go from USA "B" times to Junior Olympics or "A" times in only a single month of practice.

TIP: Keep your head in the water and breathe every three strokes! Yes, it is completely legal, as long as some small part of your head (the size of a quarter) is breaking the surface.

To further improve your time, when you do breathe, do not tilt your head up and look forward. Instead continue to look directly at the bottom as much as possible when you breathe. For some of you this is going to sound impossible, but practice it and you will soon find that not only is it possible, but it feels much better and you go much faster.

TIP: Take sneaky breaths! Look down when you breathe and lift your head as little as possible; an observer from the deck should not be able to tell when you are breathing.

One important thing to mention: When you do breast and do not take a breath every stroke, it is very important to setup in your mind ahead of time exactly when you *will* take a breath. This is because rhythm is so vitally important in both breast and fly. If you take breaths at random you are much more likely to mess up your rhythm. If you plan to take a breath every three strokes for example, you will save time and keep your rhythm.

TIP: Establish a breathing rhythm for your stroke during practice that you will use during your race.

HENRY'S STORY

It may surprise some younger swimmers to know that at one point in time there were only three main competitive strokes. Butterfly was not one of them. In fact until 1933, butterfly was essentially a form of breaststroke. Yep. That's right; butterfly and breaststroke were at one time the same stroke. How can that be? It all started at a YMCA swimming meet, with a swimmer named Henry Myers. The one thing he wanted to do was, of course, be the fastest breaststroke swimmer possible. Now I can't say what was going through his mind, but I'm guessing it may have been something like this…

Boy, I bet I could go faster if I stayed really close to the surface, that way I wouldn't be swimming as long a distance as the guys that are bobbing up and down. So that means I need to flatten my body and get my hips up and my head down. You know, I bet I could get my hands back in front of my head faster if I took them out of the water. In fact I could probably get some good speed going if I flung them around the side. Not to mention a better pull if I pulled all the way back to my hips. Surprisingly, at the time, there were no rules preventing him from swimming breaststroke in this way.

Well, this approach to breaststroke was indeed significantly faster. Henry won his meet at the YMCA, beating the favored swimmer that day. The officials were probably very confused, but after checking the rule book, they could find no reason to disqualify him. However, it so changed the stroke that the swimming community could really no longer call it breaststroke. Because it looked very much like a butterfly skimming along the water they named the new stroke the butterfly and it became an official Olympic event in 1956.

That's all well and good, but why talk about butterfly in a chapter on breaststroke? Good question! Here's a good answer: Because all of those things that went through that Olympian's head in our hypothetical example on how to make the stroke faster are still valid, and in fact it means that up to a point, breaststroke and butterfly are really the same stroke. Therefore if you are a good breaststroke swimmer, you should also be a good butterfly swimmer and the reverse is also true.

BREAK IT DOWN GRASSHOPPER

This is one case where watching the Olympians swim isn't a bad idea. Coach X often videos his swimmers at meets so that they can review the recording and look at their form. After all, how do you know what you need to work on unless you can see it? The swimmers take their video and compare it to some of the fastest swimmers around and one of the key differences you see in young or new swimmers is the lack of hips in breaststroke. Yet, if you watch the fast and experienced swimmers you see the same thing in every one of them, the hips are breaking the surface in breaststroke! This really comes as a huge surprise to many swimmers and even to some coaches!

Immediately we are asking the question why? Well, did you ever have an opportunity to watch someone break dance? There are moves like the worm, the grasshopper and many others. When you first look at them, some of these moves seem to be impossible. At the heart of these moves is a power source that not only moves your body on the dance floor, but it can also propel you down the swim lane at record speed. What is this power source? The answer is core body rotation.

Both breast and butterfly, as in break dancing, use a core body rotation along the short axis of your body. That means that you rotate around your belly button. The muscles in your abs provide a continuous source of power. The use of your hips helps to push your whole body forward for an extra shot of speed. Of course you must remember to stay shallow. If you have read the chapter on front crawl and the kinetic chain, then you will soon realize that this worm like motion is the breaststroke equivalent. By getting your hips out of the water you transfer power into fast, forward, movement. Just as in front crawl and backstroke we turned your lateral rotation into forward motion, here we turn your up/down rotation around your belly button into forward motion. That is a good thing if you want to be a *Super Sprinter!*

TIP: Use core body rotation to drive the kinetic chain

YOUR MOTHER WAS RIGHT

By now you have probably realized that body dolphin can be a very good drill for learning this rotation. If you have read the chapter on Butterfly you will be tempted to jump in and try it right now. One important difference that you must know before starting is that the body dolphin for butterfly is *not* the same body dolphin you do for breaststroke. While they are very similar, there is a change in focus. Remember all those times when your mother yelled at you for slouching? She would tell you to stand up straight and straighten your shoulders. Well, guess what? Your mother was right! When you do a body dolphin for butterfly you are focusing on getting your hips out of the water. During a breaststroke body dolphin you are focusing on getting your shoulders out of the water. You do this by shrugging your shoulders up toward your neck and then rolling them forward and back down into the water. The hips should still break the surface, but the focus is on the shoulders.

TIP: When doing body dolphin drills for breast, focus on driving with the shoulders, not the hips! Remember, the hips still need to break the surface.

PUSH IT!

Writing this section is rather difficult because there has been so much controversy regarding the hands in breaststroke. I am going to tell you in general, what seems to be a good way to do a fast and effective breaststroke "pull" and then I'm going to tell you about some small tricks based in science to go even faster. After all, as a *Super Sprinter* you are going to need to learn all your speed tricks.

First off, from this point forward we will no longer refer to the arm action as a pull. Rather, we will call it a push. This is to change your focus on what you should be doing with your hands. Many new swimmers hear that it's a pull and they will pull their hands all the way down past their hip which is illegal and will result in a disqualification.

Early in the manual you learned that one of the most important things about going fast is staying as long as possible in the water. Therefore you want to start with your hands in a tight streamline. When doing the push you will still do a mini pull, bringing your hands only to your neck or shoulders and then *push* those hands forward, straight in front of you, as fast as you possibly can!

TIP: Focus on the PUSH not the Pull.

Many years ago Coach X heard someone say that the most important thing you can possibly do with your hands in breaststroke and butterfly is absolutely nothing. After reading this chapter, you may actually start believing that yourself. For some of those reading this, you will learn that what you may have been told about a breaststroke pull isn't exactly true.

A traditional pull in breast, it turns out, isn't actually all that effective. It uses a lot of oxygen and doesn't move your body forward very far. In fact, most swimmers are pulling back so hard or pulling back so incorrectly, that they are simply slipping through the water. While this helps to warm the water and keep your opponents comfy, it doesn't do much to help you go fast. The best thing you can do with your hands is get them back out, as far as possible, in front of your head. Remember that the taller the water thinks you are, the faster you will go.

I know you are already asking how you should move your hands forward. Some of you know that by keeping your hands in the water the entire time, you continue to trick the water into thinking that you are just a little bit taller. You also reduce your form drag and thus go faster. Others of you will recognize that water is a lot thicker than air and that it resists you by the square of the force you apply to it. This means that the faster you shoot your hands forward, the harder it gets. It turns out you are both 100% correct.

As strange as that sounds, these two seemingly opposite conclusions are both at work here. So what is the solution? Again, I encourage you to do the experiment and try all three methods to see what works best for you. Hey wait – I just said all three methods! But I've only told you about two:
>   1) Recover the hands completely under the surface,
>   2) Recover the hands completely over the surface.

Well how about a compromise? Let's try this:
>   3) Recover with the hands half in and half out of the water.

That's right, recover so that two of your fingers are below the surface and two of your fingers and thumb are above the water. Now you've got the best of both worlds! Try it – it works!

OF MOLES AND OSTRICHES

Earlier in this chapter Coach X talked about why it is a bad idea to pop your head up out of the water and look around. Being a whack-a-mole is not a good idea, but being an ostrich might be. Almost everyone has, at some point in their life, seen a cartoon in which an ostrich will hide its head in the sand. While this doesn't actually happen in real life, here is one time we can actually learn something from the cartoon. When doing breast stroke, we've learned it is a really good idea to keep your arms in front of you. This is why Coach X likes to say "Push-Glide-Kick-

Glide-Repeat". Many swimmers already know this mantra, but one thing many swimmers don't seem to know is what to do with their head the whole time. The answer is, be an ostrich! To allow your arms to reach a little further and to reduce your form drag, you need to hide your head under your arms. A good way to do this is to connect your head to your hands.

That means that as you shoot your hands forward your head is moving down into the pocket created between your arms at the same time. As you reach full extension, your entire hand, even the back of your cap, should be completely under your arms. Coach X has created a neat acronym for this: HUTA. Often at meets where there are swimmers from one of Coach X's clinics you will hear team mates shouting "HUTA" from the side lines. No, it's not a bunch of military guys doing drills, nor is it a football team on the line of scrimmage. HUTA means Head Under The Arms!

TIP: When swimming breaststroke always remember HUTA: Head Under The Arms!

Remember, the longer and thinner you can make your body line in breaststroke, the faster you are going to travel. Having a great arm stroke and kick are going to be very helpful as we will see, but by staying fast in the water between the propulsion from the arms and the legs is critical. Remember that Head Under The Arms doesn't mean that you should stick your head so far down that it goes outside your body line! Stay balanced, rotate those hips and stay long to be a *Super Sprinter.*

TIP: The longer and thinner you are, the faster you will go! Keep the arms and the kick inside the body line.

THE MAGIC OF MEDUSAS

Trying to find the right way to kick can take a lot of time. Pretty much everyone agrees that you should keep your knees close together and kick out wide, around, and then together. But is this correct? There are a whole lot of very fast breaststroke swimmers that swear the best way to do it is to just push your feet straight backward. Who is right? Are they both wrong? As with any option, Coach X always recommends trying all the different approaches a few times to find what works best for you. But, rather than talk about the two approaches mentioned above, Coach X wants to talk about Medusas. No, not the mythical creatures that will turn you to stone when you look at them – here we will be talking about a jelly fish.

Now if you've ever seen a medusa swim (or any jelly fish) you will notice that it moves forward through the water. It kind of squeezes its body, pushes the water, and moves. At least that's what you would think by looking at it. But, if you film one of these guys, you will see something strange. When you put the movement into a computer and calculate the volume of water being pushed and the motion of the body to push that water, well something just doesn't add up. In fact, according to the math, the medusa should not swim forward at all! It should be moving backwards! Now that's worth taking a look at. Clearly something very strange is going on here. Somehow this sea creature is overcoming a lot of forces against it to magically move forward.

Coach X loves math, science and physics, but he also knows that not everybody else does. So he will spare you all the scientific stuff and leave you to read the studies for yourself if you are interested. While we can't get rid of all the science, I will try to make it simpler.

WAKING UP TO WAKES

You've probably seen a boat moving through the water at some point in your life. Behind the boat you no doubt saw the wake. If you are in the boat you will get an up close view of how the wake is produced. You will see that off each side of the boat there are little spirals of water that loop around and fall off behind the boat to form the outside edges of the wake. Wakes are usually shaped like a stretched out triangle and not a long rectangle. The diagonal sides of the wake are often formed by what are called vortices – those are the swirling waves that come off the boat.

You can also see this type of vortex from airplanes during some air shows. When the plane opens up a smoke canister you can see vortices form off the tips of the wings. If you haven't guessed it by now, you produce these same types of vortices when you kick in breaststroke. Off of each foot a little swirl of water will form and move back away from your body.

Well, what the medusa figured out through millions of years of evolution in the water is that if you clip off those vortices at just the right moment, something really incredible happens. You suddenly get a huge – yes, I mean HUGE – boost in your efficiency. Suddenly an action that by all accounts should be moving you backward in the water becomes so efficient that you move forward. In the case of the medusa, by breaking these vortices at just the right time it is able to gain about 60% improved efficiency in its push through the water. Let me say that again – sixty percent! Imagine if you could improve your breaststroke efficiency by 60% - wow!?

By now you are probably asking, "Okay – so *how* does the medusa do this?" Well the answer is actually quite simple. Coach X has done a lot of research and found that the medusa is not the only sea creature that learned this trick. In fact just about every fast aquatic animal has figured it out. Did you ever notice the odd shape of the tail fin of many fish? Did you notice that it doesn't just go straight back behind them? It tapers up and down. You may also have noticed, without realizing it, that the size of the tail fin always seems to be the same with respect to the rest of the fish – no matter what type of fast moving fish you look at. Why you can even look at lobsters and see a similar design. Have you figured out the secret yet?

It turns out that the medusa has evolved so that its base (head) is exactly ¼ the size of its body length. Or put another way, it is exactly 4 times longer than it is wide. Now if you happen to have access to a fish (and please don't pull one out of your sister's fish tank – that just wouldn't be a good idea), measure the length of the tail from top to bottom and then measure the length of the fish from nose to tail. Surprised? That's right; the ratio is exactly 1:4. It turns out that this is a somewhat magical ratio when it comes to vortices in water. In animals that have evolved this magic ratio, they are able to break their vortices off the tips of their bodies and gain an enormous boost in speed and power because of it.

Now let me tell you how you can use this knowledge to become a *Super Sprinter*. All you need to do is measure your body length. Now remember you are going to be very long and streamlined when doing breaststroke – right? So make sure that when you measure your height, you measure from tip toes to pointy fingertip. Now divide that number by 4. A calculator may be required, but here is a simple experiment to do this in the pool.

USING A LANE AS A MEASURING STICK

By yourself or with a friend, line yourself up against the lane line. Position your pointed toes at the start of one buoy on the lane line. Now, count the number of buoys from your toes to your fingertips. Divide this number by 4. You can do this easily in the pool by figuring out half the distance in buoys and then taking half of that distance again. Now, align your feet to the buoys so that you are lying across the lane, between the two ropes of the lane lines. Separate your feet by the number of buoys you just got from your calculations above, and that is exactly how wide you should be kicking – no more, no less.

TIP: Ensure your breaststroke kick is exactly ¼ as wide as your body is long to get a 60% improvement in efficiency and a huge increase in speed!

If you don't hit that magic 1:4 ratio you will not get the boost. Once you know how wide it is, practice it. Believe me; you will know it when you find it. You will suddenly feel yourself moving noticeably further with each kick even though you are using the exact same amount of kicking power.

One more thing to help master this: If you happen to have some rope or elastic stretch cord, you may be able to fashion something that you can place around your ankles. Cut the cord so that the width is exactly the required length. Then attach the cord around your ankles so that it is impossible for you to kick any wider than your optimal kicking width. After you practice like this for a while, the correct width will become a habit and you will no longer require the cord.

Keep in mind that this technique is only for swimmers on their way to becoming *Super Sprinters*. If you've not yet mastered your breaststroke kick or figured out what works best for you (traditional frog kick or straight back kick and squeeze), then you may want to get that down solid before refining the width of your kick. The one thing most swimmers report is that they are surprised at how narrow their kick becomes, yet they can travel the same speed. That's actually a really good thing! It means you end up using less energy to travel just as fast and therefore have more energy than your opponent when you need it. In addition you may find yourself going much further before you begin to tire during a race.

DIAMONDS IN THE WATER

We are down to one last major element of the stroke. So far we have talked about the critical importance of balance, how to get speed and distance from rotation, why reaching and gliding will improve your time and we discussed how to use a more efficient and propulsive kick. It seems the final item on our list should be a discussion about the arms. Earlier in the chapter we said that there are those who feel the best thing you can do with your arms in this stroke is nothing at all. By now, you may already agree with them. Let's look a little deeper into the science behind the arm stroke.

We've all seen young swimmers do breaststroke. Sometimes, it sure doesn't look pretty. Most of the time new swimmers have their head out of the water the entire time. They look around and pull their arms all the way down to their hips. There is actually some good science around why this is so. As land based animals we generally like to breathe and given that we don't have gills, it shouldn't be any surprise as to why so many new swimmers keep their head out of the water. It's more natural for us to do it that way. Similarly, we have evolved to use our sense of sight as our primary means to navigate the world. It is very awkward for us to be moving forward and not look in that direction. Finally, on land when we want to move forward, we push backward with our feet and legs. We have learned that by pushing hard on something we will move opposite that direction. The more we push, the further we move. If we want to climb up on something we can use our arms and push ourselves up.

GRPAHITE IS FOREVER

One of Coach X's favorite classes ever was biophysical chemistry. You take everything you've ever learned about calculus, physics, organic chemistry and biology and combine them all into one class. Here's an example of how awesome this class was: On the very first day students had to calculate how many breaths it would take to inhale one atom of argon exhaled by Julius Caesar when he took his last breath. If you got the answer wrong you were dropped from the class. Coach X got it right!

One of the really neat things about biophysical chemistry is that we got to look at phase diagrams for all sorts of elements. Did you know that there is more than one form of ice? The other great thing is finding that all forms of carbon eventually, under normal earthly conditions, revert to graphite – even diamonds! As the professor said, to get your special someone something that will truly last forever, ditch the diamonds and go for a mechanical pencil!

Hopefully Coach X has now got you wondering why in the world he is telling you all of this stuff about diamonds and graphite in a chapter on breaststroke. Read on and all will be explained.

Imagine doing a breaststroke arm pull. What does that look like? One popular way that breaststroke is taught is to make a "Y" with your arms on the surface, then drop the arms to make a diamond shape in the water. When you do this you are setting up your arms for maximal force. Your elbow is high and the arms are bent. But then what? If you pull backward your arm will immediately go past the point where it makes maximum force. Your arm will straighten out and you'll get almost no power.

ARE YOU AN ILLEGAL WATER HEATER?

The solution for many swimmers is to continue pulling backward all the way down to their suit. That's not just bad because it's illegal and will get you disqualified; it's bad because science shows that you are just wasting your energy. Once your arms lose that nice ninety degree bend you just don't have enough strength to effectively push your body forward. All you are really doing is spending energy to warm up the water. Not good.

Ah ha, you say, but I'm smarter than that, I don't pull backward. You are a breaststroke pro and you bring your arms up to your face. Keeping in mind that we only move when we direct water in the opposite direction, Coach X doesn't think you will have any trouble figuring out that pulling your arms up toward your face isn't going to make you move forward.

This all means that, for most breaststroke swimmers, the only propulsive portion of the arm stroke is when you transition your arms from the "Y" to the diamond. That is a considerably shorter time than most swimmers realize. To make matters worse, many breaststroke swimmers do not drop their hands and keep their elbows high. Instead they drop their elbows and slide them backward in the water. If you are doing this; stop!

TIP: Never drop your elbows and slide them backwards! You have no power on the water in this position.

When you drop your elbows you are just sliding your arms through the water without applying any pressure. In other words, your pull is just wasting energy, it's not moving you forward very much (or possibly even at all). To get the most out of your arms, keep the elbows high, near the surface of the water.

TIP: Keep elbow high, near the surface! This is the correct anchoring for the breaststroke.

CHARLIE'S STORY

Many swimmers from around the world often contact Coach X to review their strokes and to get advice on how to improve their times. Generally Coach X gets videos from swimmers a few months before a major swim meet and will review the videos and send them back with an audio commentary. A number of years ago, Coach X received a phone call fairly late one afternoon. The person on the other end of the phone identified himself as a swimmer from Iowa who had attended one of Coach X's clinics. His name was Charlie. He said that he had a state meet the next day and he needed to drop three seconds in the 100 breaststroke the next day!

Talk about pressure! Coach X told Charlie that it was next to impossible to do anything that dramatic in a single day. Charlie was persistent to say the least. While on the phone he uploaded a video to Coach X's website. After quickly reviewing the video, it was obvious that Charlie's coach never watched how Charlie swam during practice, or at least never corrected his arm stroke. Charlie was already a very fast breaststroke swimmer or he would not have made it to the state high school championships. However, he was sliding his elbows backward and not getting any pressure on the "Y" to diamond conversion. In other words, his arm pull was almost completely ineffective. His speed primarily came from his kick, long body and awesome streamline.

Coach X realized that dropping three seconds in this case would actually be quite easy. In a few minutes Coach X made a video demonstrating the correct arm technique and posted it for Charlie to download. After watching the video, Charlie went to a local indoor pool and practiced keeping his elbow high. Later that night he called back and reported that he felt like he was going significantly faster. The swim meet was the next day and Coach X was dying to know what happened. Eventually the phone call came. Charlie's mom was on the phone and she was ecstatic. She told Coach X that Charlie did not drop three seconds. This seemed confusing as she sounded excited, but her son apparently didn't achieve the time drop he wanted. She next said, "Coach, he dropped seven seconds and came in first place!" Ah yes, the power of the high elbow should not be underestimated! Imagine that, seven seconds in a 100 breast overnight just from fixing the elbows in the arm pull, now that's a true *Super Sprinter!*

IF IT FEELS RIGHT

Normally Coach X has a saying that goes like this, "If when you swim, something doesn't feel right, then it probably isn't." But sometimes the reverse is also true. There are times when something feels just perfect to you, but it just isn't right. A great example of this is swimmers that do their arm pull with their elbows at or behind their shoulders.

When you start your breaststroke pull with your elbows at your shoulders you are setting yourself up for disaster. You can even demonstrate this while you are sitting down and reading this book! If you bring your elbows to your shoulders, then try to drop your hands and squeeze your elbows, you will notice something bad. Your elbows come right to your sides like chicken wings. That's right; it forces you to drop your elbows! Worse, you can't really squeeze them because they are up against your sides.

Coach X will tell you a much better way in a moment, but for now, just know that you should never start your pull when your elbows are at your shoulders. It may feel fast, but it is actually very slow.

TIP: Never start your breaststroke pull with your elbows at your shoulders! It forces you to drop your elbows and lose your anchor.

MEANWHILE, BACK TO THE GRAPHITE

Nope, Coach X did not forget that earlier in this chapter he started talking to you about diamonds and graphite. Coach X said he would tell you what that was all about later, and guess what; it's later!

Okay, so what the heck was Coach X talking about? The problem with pulling to the diamond position is that too many swimmers either do it wrong by pulling too far or spend too much time there by pulling up to their face. Remember from earlier in the chapter we learned the importance of being long and being balanced. It's very important to start your stroke long and balanced and to finish your stroke long and balanced. By some accounts you should be spending over ninety percent of your time in that long, balanced, streamline position. The trick then is to complete the pull as efficiently and quickly as possible. In other words, diamonds are not forever! Don't hold that diamond position, rather get back to a streamline as quickly as possible and make that your "graphite" position.

TIP: Favor the streamline position in breaststroke

See, Coach X told you this would all start to make sense. You may be wondering if Coach X is going to give you some new, cool, trick to help you out. Answer: You bet! Keep in mind that if you are already a swimmer who is not having any difficulty in doing a "Y" to diamond conversion, keeping your elbows high and getting back to streamline quickly; then this section may not pertain to you.

As an alternative to fully dropping your arms down to the bottom, then sweeping in and up to your face and lunging forward, consider the following: Use the science you have learned so far.

To ensure you have high elbows and maintain a proper anchor on the water, keep your elbows well out in front of your shoulders. Some coaches call this a mini scull. While the name may be mini, the power is great. When your elbows are out in front of the shoulders, simply scull the hands out, down and around. The faster you can get your hands back to the streamline position, the faster you will go.

When practiced and done well, this arm pull is a perfect replacement for the traditional breaststroke pull. The trick is, keep your elbows high the entire time. Only the sculling hands will drop below the elbows. As the hands scull and the arms squeeze you will be providing energy to move you quickly through the water. The mini-pull keeps your elbows high on the water the entire time, thus increasing the amount of power you can apply to the water. By sculling the hands instead of fully dropping the arms, you avoid pulling past the ninety degree point and losing power. In addition, you are able to keep a more constant connection to the water as you apply pressure in the direction of movement. This means less energy is wasted pushing side to side or up and down. Finally, the min-pull allows you to get your arms back to a streamline much more quickly than the traditional breaststroke pull. This mini-pull encompasses all of the scientific approaches to improving your speed. By the way, in the story above, the video that Coach X sent to Charlie was demonstrating a high elbow mini-pull which resulted in a seven second time drop overnight.

TIP: Replace your traditional breaststroke pull with a mini-scull pull for better power and speed!

BREASTSTROKE TIP SUMMARY

GENERAL

TIP: Swim breaststroke using the mantra: Push – Glide, Kick – Glide

TIP: Always know this: You are your own best coach! Validate everything you are told.

BALANCE

TIP: Proper balance is critical in breaststroke! Stay level during each stroke when gliding.

TIP: Balance level during the glide. Shooting out of the water at an angle adds significant drag.

ROTATION

TIP: Use core body rotation to drive the kinetic chain

TIP: When doing body dolphin drills for breast, focus on driving with the shoulders, not the hips! Remember, the hips still need to break the surface.

DRAG / RESISTANCE

TIP: Stay very shallow in breaststroke to avoid forcing your body to the surface on every stroke.

TIP: Diving too deep in breast actually increases the distance you have to swim and will kill your time. Favor a very small amplitude (up and down motion) when doing breaststroke!

TIP: Get under the wake! Your hips should pass underneath the small wake you create in front of your body when you dive underwater.

TIP: Optimize how far you travel under water during the glide! You should start the next stroke or kick before you start to slow down.

TIP: The longer and thinner you are, the faster you will go! Keep the arms and the kick inside the body line.

TIP: Favor the streamline position in breaststroke

PULL

TIP: Focus on the PUSH not the Pull.

TIP: Never drop your elbows and slide them backwards! You have no power on the water in this position.

TIP: Keep elbow high, near the surface! This is the correct anchoring for the breaststroke.

TIP: Never start your breaststroke pull with your elbows at your shoulders! It forces you to drop your elbows and lose your anchor.

TIP: Replace your traditional breaststroke pull with a mini-scull pull for better power and speed!

KICK

TIP: Ensure your breaststroke kick is exactly ¼ as wide as your body is long to get a 60% improvement in efficiency and a huge increase in speed!

HEAD / BREATHING

TIP: Keep your head in the water and breathe every three strokes! Yes, it is completely legal, as long as some small part of your head (the size of a quarter) is breaking the surface.

TIP: Take sneaky breaths! Look down when you breathe and lift your head as little as possible; an observer from the deck should not be able to tell when you are breathing.

TIP: Establish a breathing rhythm for your stroke during practice that you will use during your race.

TIP: When swimming breaststroke always remember HUTA: Head Under The Arms!

BUTTERFLY

"Employ your time in improving yourself by other men's writings, so that you shall gain easily what others have labored hard for."

Socrates

BUTTERFLY

As you might have expected, Coach X has saved the best for last. If we could somehow set up a poll and ask people how many of you skipped right to this chapter, Coach X is willing to be that it would be a very low number. That's because, of all the strokes, butterfly definitely gets the worst rap. Every swimmer has heard stories or knows from personal experience how horribly painful this stoke can be. Many swimmers refer to the stroke as "butterstruggle", and in fact, for many swimmers, that's exactly what it is. How many of you reading this handbook right now would believe me, if I were to tell you that butterfly is in fact one of the easiest of all the strokes to swim and that it is in fact one of the most efficient strokes to swim? Probably not many.

FORGET ABOUT BUTTERSTRUGGLE

The biggest problem with butterfly has nothing to do with swimming, but rather with coaching. If you were one of the fortunate few to have had a coach that knows how to teach butterfly correctly, you are very lucky indeed. Many year round programs do a fair job of it, but in high school and in recreation leagues as well as lessons, you are for the most part, out of luck!

This reminds Coach X of a time when he was visiting a YMCA near Milwaukee, Wisconsin. This particular YMCA had several very nice indoor pools and had a great reputation as having one of the best swim teams in the state. Interestingly most of the really good swimmers on the team were not originally from the YMCA. This was interesting to Coach X because this YMCA also offered several levels of lesson programs for young swimmers which ended with them joining the year round team.

On the day that Coach X visited, it was time for the swimmers to learn butterfly. In one pool an instructor was giving butterfly lessons. Before the lesson, she came over to another instructor and asked for help because she did not know how to teach butterfly. Unfortunately it seemed the other instructor did not know either! But that certainly is not what they told their class. The new instructor simply said that he had always hated fly and so he never really learned it either. Keep in mind that both of these instructors were WSI certified instructors – which meant, at least in theory, that they demonstrated the ability to teach butterfly during their training. Finally they collaborated and decided that it couldn't be that hard after all and they showed the kids how to kick about and move their arms. Watching the kids try to swim in this manner was a sorry sight indeed.

Coach X wonders how many of them went on to join the swimming team after that? Reality is that butterfly, when taught right and swam correctly, is actually a very efficient and relaxing stroke. So, let's break it down and figure out what makes us go through the water when we swim this stroke.

TIP: Don't over complicate butterfly! Think of it as body dolphin with arms.

First question – what are we trying to do? Well, we are trying to move on the surface of the water. That's simple enough but that definition seems to work for all the strokes. What makes butterfly different? Well to start with, we will not be on our side at any time during the stroke. We will instead remain pretty much on our stomach. This makes the stroke very different from both front crawl and backstroke. It also makes it very similar to breaststroke. So much so, that your times in both butterfly and breaststroke should be very close to one another. If they aren't – you know that you are swimming at least one of the strokes incorrectly.

BALANCING ACT

Science tells us that the single most important thing in all of swimming, the one thing that you absolutely need to know; is balance. It seems strange, but it's true. Think about it. You could be the number one butterfly swimmer in the world, be able to bench press more than anyone else, have a greater lung capacity than anyone else in the world, but you simply are not going to move an inch if your body is vertical in the water! Learning to balance properly in the water is the first step in doing any stroke correctly. Let's take a look at what science tells us about being properly balanced in this stroke.

Remember when you were very little (and for some of you that may be right now!) and you played on a see-saw. It certainly wasn't much fun to play on it all alone. You would just crash down and hurt yourself on the ground while the other side would spring up into the air. Yet, that is exactly how most swimmers try to balance when they swim butterfly. Which is to say; not at all! To get the see-saw balanced you need to have a friend that can sit on the other seat. Hopefully your friend is about the same weight as you or you are still going to have problems. One person will crash down while the other is catapulted into the sky. As you already know, you can still balance the see-saw when one person is bigger than the other. Some cool new see-saws actually allow you to move the center part and change the pivot point! Doing this changes the center of balance so that you are both able to rock gently up and down.

Rocking up and down should make you think of something else. Perhaps a stroke called butterfly. If it does, that's very good for you. If not, keep reading and it will soon make sense. It turns out that your body is a lot like that see-saw. You want it to balance flat on the water as much as possible. But like a see-saw with a big kid and a little kid, there is an imbalance in the system. In this case think of your legs as the great big kid and your head as the little kid. You can think of your lungs as the balance point of the see-saw. If you do nothing at all, the big kid is going to come crashing down to the ground, and indeed if you simply float face down in the water you will quickly feel your legs begin to sink as your body begins to move into a vertical position. This is not balance!

TIP: To remain balanced in fly requires you put more pressure on your chest and face to get your hips up.

To fix this situation you will need to put some more force on the head (little kid) side of the see-saw. This means that you must press your face, neck and shoulders down into the water. Notice

I did not say *push* your face into the water, We don't want you to go too deep, all you need to do is press; as in put more pressure on your face, neck and shoulders. You can try this and practice it and you will notice that your hips will magically come to the surface of the water. This is good! But do remember not to go too deep in the water with your head. In fact when you do it really well, you should still have a very small (dime size) amount of your head still breaking the surface. When balancing correctly, your shoulder blades should also be breaking the surface, and your hips should definitely be breaking the surface.

HOW TO KICK ON YOUR STOMACH

A very good drill to start with when learning proper balance for butterfly and for breaststroke is to simply kick on your stomach without a board. Keep your arms at your side and look *straight down* at the bottom of the pool. Don't worry about hitting your head on the wall; that's what those targets are for on the bottom of the pool. When you see the black T you know you are near the wall. Have a friend or coach watch you from the deck. Of course, Coach X always recommends using a video camera if you have one handy. Have your observer watch as you kick to ensure that three things are breaking the surface as you flutter kick. The observer should see the back of your head just breaking the surface, your shoulder blades, and your hips (or briefs) must break the surface at all times. If the observer reports that your hips are under water, then you need to put more pressure on your face and your chest. Push down and your suit will pop right out. Get used to this feeling and keep that sense of balance as you go into your body dolphin.

Now that you have figured out how to balance, let's figure out how to move through the water.

TIP: Use the rule of three: Three things must break the surface, the back of your head, your shoulders, then your hips or briefs in that order.

DRAGONS EELS AND MERMAIDS

Once we have learned balance, we are well on our way to swimming an effortless butterfly. Science shows us that rotation is the next most important thing to think about. This is because the majority of our propulsive force in butterfly, what makes us move in the water, comes from body rotation. Now you are probably thinking one of two things. Some of you are saying, "Wait just a minute! You just said the major propulsive force in butterfly is my rotation. What about my arms?" As it turns out, Coach X has done a pretty fun experiment over and over again and generally gets the same results regardless of the swimmer's level of experience. Go ahead and try this experiment for yourself:

NO ARM BUTTERFLY

Hop in the pool and have a coach or friend time you as you do a 25 yard body dolphin as fast as you can. Try to avoid taking breaths if possible and remember – absolutely no arms. To make things more interesting you can try this with your arms at your side for one length, and then repeat with the arms in front. Next, do a timed regular 25 yard butterfly.

The results surprise most swimmers. In almost all cases, you will go several seconds faster doing the 25 yard body dolphin versus doing the full stroke with arms. To find out why, keep reading.

TIP: Where your hands go, your body will follow. Place the hands on the surface; do not claw into the water.

The other half of you are probably saying, "Wait Just a Minute! There can't be any rotation in butterfly; you need to stay on your stomach. Just what are you talking about!?" And, yes, of course you are right. Well, at least about the part where you need to stay on your stomach. But butterfly, as well as breaststroke, both *do* have a rotation. It's just not down the length of your body; it's across the width of your body. Basically you are going to be rotating up and down over your belly button!

POP YOUR BUTTONS

One very effective way to drive your hips is by "popping" your belly button. It's a little like becoming a belly dancer in the water. Essentially what you want to do is pull in your stomach and push in your belly button. We call this popping the belly button because it should be done very quickly and as you do it, you will rotate your hips. The effect is like setting up a small spring in your body that gets released as you push your hips back down into the water and glide. The key here is to glide. Most swimmers forget this and just continue to pop their belly button and waste energy. At the end of each pulse of your body dolphin wave, there should be a short glide before you start the next cycle.

TIP: Pop your belly button to drive your hip rotation and setup an efficient body dolphin.

REPLACING YOUR CAR ENGINE USING YOUR WIPER MOTOR

There is an analogy that Coach X has heard so many times he has forgotten where he originally heard it. But since it is a good analogy and makes the point, it is well worth repeating here. Imagine a really fast sports car. Ok, got it? Good. Now imagine one even faster than that!

Imagine this car has one of the world's most powerful engines under the hood. Many of you would love to be behind the wheel of that car! I'm sure you can picture yourself racing down the road at top speed listening to the hum of the well-tuned engine. Now imagine that someone has "fixed" the car so that it turns the wheels not by using that powerful engine under the hood, but instead it will now turn the wheels using the windshield wiper motor!

This sounds pretty ridiculous I know. But yet, that is what nearly every butterfly swimmer has done! Rather than using their extremely powerful engine (their abs and hips), they choose instead to use the comparably tiny little muscles in their arms and knees (windshield wiper motors). At least in humans it is not nearly as bad as it would be for the car, but very nearly so!

RED, WHITE AND YOU

You see the muscles in your knees and elbows (even if you are the buffest of all swimmers on your team) are very small and get tired very fast when compared to the muscles in your abs. The muscles in your abs are called Type I or slow-twitch red fiber muscles. They are designed to go the long haul. The muscles in your elbows and especially in your knees were not designed for continuous output – they do a much better job at short sprint motions than they do at long term velocity driven movements.

TIP: The muscles in your knees and arms are Type II, short-twitch white fibers and are not designed for long term power output. They will give out quickly if you rely on them in butterfly.

If you are using only your arms or knees to swim in butterfly you are in for a lot of misery. You will get tired *very* fast. In addition, because the muscles in your knees and elbows are not as efficient as your abdominal muscles, you will use all your oxygen and you will start to hurt. When the oxygen is gone, those arm and leg muscles will start to function in an anaerobic state; a much less efficient method by far and one that produces lactic acid. It is lactic acid that makes your muscles hurt so badly. So for all of these reasons, swimming butterfly primarily with your elbows and knees is just not a good idea.

TIP: Your abs are built for long lasting power! Use them instead of your knees and arms to provide power during butterfly.

QUICK, TO THE FISH TANK!

The solution is very simple. To solve our problem we need to take a look at nature. Watching fish swim is very useful for us as swimmers. Since fish are native to the aquatic environment, and we as land based mammals are not, we can very often learn a great deal by watching how fish swim. Looking at any fish you will immediately see that they have two tiny fins near their gills that look like tiny little arms. One thing that is immediately apparent with even the humblest of goldfish is that they do not use their tiny little fins to propel their bodies through the water! How do they do it? They wiggle! That's right – watch any fish from a flounder to a shark and you will see the same mode of propulsion – wiggling through the stream. So now that you think about it – doesn't it just seem silly to think that you can really go fast in butterfly by using your tiny little fins (I mean arms)? To get solid propulsion from butterfly you are going to need to wiggle.

TIP: Drive your butterfly propulsion with your rotation, not with your arms!

THE SWIMMER FROM ATLANTIS

Because Coach X does not want to favor boys over girls or vice versa, he has something for everyone to imagine when they swim. For young boys, try to imagine that your body is the tail of a dragon; older boys may want to imagine that they are a giant eel or break dancing the worm. Young girls can think of themselves as a mermaid and older girls – well, I haven't come up with anything yet, but if you do, let me know! For you to wiggle through the water as a human and get some really nice propulsion have a friend watch you as you go through the water. Here are a couple of things to remember.

First, you should not use your arms or your legs when you practice your body rotation, you should only be wiggling up and down in the water. Next, make sure that you are looking straight down at the bottom of the pool. Remember that lifting your head even a little bit will have very big effect on sinking your hips. To avoid this, look down at all times, even when you breathe. Okay, now you have the basics. All that is left is to have your buddy watch you from the deck. Tell her to look for three things. You want the back of your head to break the surface, followed by your shoulder blades and finally your hips. The hips should come out slightly higher than either your head or your shoulders.

Keep in mind that you don't want any two surfaces to break at the same time. Instead you want to have a wave roll through your body. The wave should resemble the path a dolphin makes when jumping through the water. That is why this wiggle motion in humans is referred to as body dolphin. Just remember that unlike a dolphin, you don't want to go high or deep during your body dolphin, instead try to stay as close to the surface as possible.

TIP: The deeper you go, the longer the pool becomes and the slower your time.

Once you master this rotation you will find that your butterfly has already become much easier and more efficient. You are literally halfway to a far more efficient stroke. Start off very slow with this. Do many repetitions as a drill and continue until you feel that you really have both balance and rotation. Remember that your buddy should see all three items (head, shoulders, and hips) every time your body pulses through the water like a wave of energy. If she does not, chances are that you are going too deep into the water. The trick is to stay shallow.

VERTICAL TAKEOFF

If you are still finding it difficult to master a nice even rhythm when doing your body dolphin, Coach X has a great suggestion for you. Go to the deep end of the pool, place your hands at your sides and begin to push just the front or your hips or briefs forward, then push your butt backward, then push forward again. Do not bend your knees. Do this until you can stay above water comfortably. Next, do this with both arms above your head. Once you can again stay above water, slowly lean forward and change from vertical (straight up and down) to horizontal (on the surface of the pool) and keep going. You will find that you are now doing an almost perfect body dolphin on the surface!

TIP: If you are having trouble mastering body dolphin, start from a vertical body dolphin in the deep end.

FORWARD AND BACKWARD

In his swimming clinics, Coach X has met many swimmers that *think* they have mastered the body dolphin. However, many of these swimmers are still bending their knees. The trick to doing a proper body dolphin in butterfly is to *never* bend the knees. Let Coach X say that again; *never*, never bend the knees! Instead curve your legs and allow the wave action to flow from your hips all the way out your toes.

TIP: Never bend your knees in fly; curve your legs and allow the wave to flow from your hips out your toes!

To see if you've truly mastered body dolphin for butterfly, try this simple test: swim it backwards! That's right; do your body dolphin so that you move feet first. If you have truly mastered body dolphin, you should be able to go almost as fast backward as you can forward. But if you are bending your knees, you will find this task almost impossible!

TIP: If you have truly mastered body dolphin for butterfly, you should be able to body dolphin backwards almost as fast as forwards!

THE CLAW!

Now that you have mastered the balance and rotation of the stroke we must address the next most common problem: the arms. Many swimmers do the butterfly stroke using mostly human struggle skills; they do not make the stroke very relaxing. Just watch a new butterfly swimmer enter the water with their arms. It looks very much like they are attacking the water by clawing or shoveling into it. This can lead to may problems.

To begin with, remember that where your hands go, your body will follow. Since we know that it's most efficient to swim at the surface of the water we certainly don't want to be directing our hands to the bottom! If you attack the water and jab down into it with your clawing hands, your body is going to follow that same path. This means that you are very likely to go far too deep and slow down your speed. That's not what a *Super Sprinter* wants to do at all; we are all about speed! For now, let's just agree that we do not want to be jabbing or clawing into the water.

TIP: Do not claw into the water; this will cause you to dive too deep! Keep your arms straight during a butterfly recovery.

A better approach is to think about simply placing your hands on the water as far out in front of you as possible. Remember, as discussed in the other chapters, the longer you are, the less drag there will be on your body. The less drag, the faster you go. By reaching those arms forward instead of bending them and entering short, you will be dropping seconds from your time.

TIP: The further you stretch your arms in front of your head, the less drag on your body and the faster you go!

AMANDA'S STORY

Coach X likes to share stories about fast swimmers with you. It helps to understand what other people had to go through to become a *Super Sprinter*. This is a story that Coach X wishes he did not have to tell, but it contains a very important lesson. So, please read it and learn from it so that you can become a *Super Sprinter* for the long term and hopefully not repeat what happened here.

There was a swimmer that Coach X knew for many years, her name was Amanda. In fact, Coach X actually taught her how to swim when she was very little. Amanda became a very good swimmer on her year round team, but the team was not very large and Amanda was looking for more competition. She was a very fast butterfly swimmer and there were not too many swimmers of her caliber on her current team. Amanda's parents asked the team coach her thoughts on Amanda moving to another team. The coach said that she understood Amanda's concern and recommended several nearby coaches. She also warned Amanda's parents about another very popular team nearby.

The other team was known as one of the best teams in the area and had even collected several outstanding gold level awards from USA swimming. It was a very large team with well over 300 swimmers. It was true that they turned out some fast athletes, but it also had a reputation among local coaches as being a swimmer mill. They just didn't care much about the swimmers; they were only interested in times. Amanda's coach was aware of several swimmers that went to this other team to improve their fly and required shoulder surgery before age fifteen. For this reason she strongly cautioned Amanda's parents to consider a different team.

Amanda's parents did consider other teams, but in the end they were lured by the fact that the big team was very popular and producing national level swimmers. They wanted Amanda to be one of them. As it turned out Amanda was already placing in the top ten at all her meets, but the parents felt that she could do even better if she trained with the larger team and the award winning coaches.

Amanda moved to the new team. She loved the competition from all the new swimmers in her lane. She quickly moved up the lane hierarchy and started to get her senior qualifying times. After a few years she was consistently placing in the top eight at the senior level meets and even qualifying for national level meets. She was doing very well and was quickly gaining the attention of interested colleges.

As she was also an outstanding student, Amanda received a swimming scholarship to a very good university. She was thrilled! After talking things over with her parents, Amanda accepted the scholarship and attended the university as a freshman. That year she did very well, again placing in the top eight at nearly every meet. However, her college coach noticed problems with Amanda's butterfly recovery. It was the same thing that Amanda's old coach had warned her about before she moved to the new team. Her college coach became very concerned when Amanda started complaining of shoulder pain.

At each practice Amanda would complain that something did not feel right in her shoulder. The college coach would point out that this was because she was swimming fly wrong. She was breathing at the wrong time and lifting her arm too high. Amanda said that her first coach had told her that and was working on it, but when she went to the big team, they never mentioned it. As a result it became habit. Even though she became very fast with that technique, it was wrong!

By the end of the season, Amanda was no longer placing in the top eight at any meets. Finally the coach had to have a serious conversation with Amanda and informed her that they had to pull her scholarship. In addition, the doctor told her that she absolutely had to have surgery to repair the damage on her shoulder. To heal she would need to take some time off from school and out of the pool.

Coach X is happy to say that Amanda is now back in school and back in the pool. She is recovering slowly, and although she no longer has her scholarship, she is working her way back into the top eight thanks to her college coach who is once again teaching her the right way to swim butterfly.

There are many things to take away from this story. Do not be lured to a big team just because there are more swimmers there. Do not be lured to a team because they have USA Swimming recognition. If they have many swimmers it is almost a given that they will have many awards. It does not mean that the coaches are any good.

There are approximately 300,000 USA-S swimmers and approximately 3,590 spots at Olympic Trials. That means that on average 1 in 83 swimmers will make it to trials. If Amanda's new team had nearly 400 swimmers, the coaches should have been taking five swimmers to trials. More accurately they should have taken five spots at Olympic Trials meaning one swimmer could qualify for multiple events. But this was not the case. Each of the three qualifying swimmers only qualified in one event.

The math indicates that the coaches on Amanda's new team were likely hindering swimmers from achieving their best times. But these factors are not considered when making awards. USA swimming simply looks at the total numbers. Large teams almost invariably get these awards with the idea that it is due to good coaching. The reality is that most swimmers will do better on smaller teams, provided there are still enough swimmers to challenge them and do relays. A team with only twenty swimmers that sends one person to trials every four Olympics (sixteen years) is statistically doing better than Amada's team that is sending three swimmers every four years!

Coach X does not mean to belittle the USA-S team recognition system. He will be the first to point out that very few teams across the nation qualify for gold award status. Coach X simply questions whether the criteria being used truly makes valid sense. How many smaller teams and coaches are going unrecognized because of these award programs? The biggest issue Coach X has with these programs is that it tends to drive swimmers to the bigger teams and perpetuates the problem. This is not always the case though. Coach X is also aware of several very excellent gold level teams across the nation that he would personally recommend.

One more thing about this story; Coach X is very aware of the team in this story and knows seven other swimmers who swam there and required shoulder surgery before age seventeen. He is also aware of one boy who was also originally on Amanda's team who also switched to the larger team. This boy already had Olympic Trial times while on his old team. After six months on the larger team, he quit swimming altogether because they pushed him too hard.

Guess what; he too required shoulder surgery. Coach X was stunned that an Olympic quality swimmer would completely give up the sport due to poor coaching. So, Coach X urges all of you *Super Sprinters*; rather than switching to a new team, make your team the one you want it to be. Get your friends involved and your teammates. If you want a bigger team, make it bigger! Own it. Regardless of the team size, if you have a great coach, keep them! On the other hand, if you are on a big team now and your coach is just making you do laps; maybe it is time to find a smaller team!

TIP: Be careful not to overdue butterfly. If you feel pain in your shoulder notify your coach immediately; it means you are doing something wrong!

IT'S THE BUTTERFLY, NOT THE DOVE

How you get your hands in front of you is just as important as what you do once they get there. It's true that too many fly swimmers bend their elbows and claw at the water, but many also try to lift their arms straight up out of the water like a dove wing. If you are doing this type of a recovery; stop! Besides not being an efficient recovery method, this could actually cause shoulder injuries over time! Coach X has seen far too many swimmers end up requiring shoulder surgery at a young age because they, or their coaches, did not pay attention to this warning. To help, use this experiment in simple human anatomy:

TIP: When doing a fly recovery it is important to keep your arms low and straight.

BOOING BUTTERFLY

Here's another experiment that you can do out of the pool. Simply stand up and hold both of your arms out to the side at shoulder height. Keep your palms facing down. Next, with your arms straight out to the side; turn your thumbs down like you are booing this experiment. Then rotate your thumbs backward so they point behind you. Finally move your arms forward while holding your hands in this position. While you do this, notice that it is impossible to bend your elbows!

The arms can be kept straight by simply locking the elbow. After all, if you don't have an elbow, you can't bend your arm, right? Better yet, you can't bend your elbow during a butterfly recovery if your thumbs are pointing down and behind you during the race.

This solves the problem of bending, clawing, or not fully extending your arms during a butterfly recovery. The simple act of rotating your thumbs backward will greatly improve your arm recovery and dramatically improve your times.

The key here is to keep them pointed down or backward during the *entire* recovery. Many swimmers start with their thumbs down or backward and end up with the thumbs up or forward by the time their hands are in front of their heads, so watch out for that! Keep the thumbs down or slightly backwards the entire time. This will ensure that your arms are straight and make for good placement of the hands on the water at the end of the recovery.

TIP: Turn your thumbs down or backward during the recovery to lock your elbows and guarantee a straight arm recovery!

UP, UP AND AWAY – NO WAY!

As we said above, another common mistake among new fly swimmers is the attempt to lift the arms up out of the water and as high as possible into the air. Not only is this extremely inefficient, it is a very good way to get hurt! Shoulders were not designed to do that, and with very little repetition, you are setting yourself up for a major shoulder injury and possibly even surgery down the road. Let's stop this practice right here and now. Arms in butterfly are meant to go around the body on the surface of the water (just above skimming the surface). The best description that Coach X can give is that you should make a "snow angel" in the water. Coach X refers to these as "water angels".

ANGELS IN THE WATER

Here is a very good drill that you can use to help learn how to extend your arms as far as possible in front of your head while also learning a nice low sweep. It's a drill Coach X calls "water angels". For those of you who grew up in cold climates, you should have no problem figuring out this next drill. Just imagine doing a snow angel on the surface of the water with only your arms. Here is how it works. Start by doing the balance drill you learned at the beginning of the chapter where you flutter kick on your stomach with arms at your sides. As you kick, very slowly begin to move your arms toward the front of your body. Just skim the surface of the water with your arms, don't try to pull them out of the water yet, and don't let them go under water either. Remember to keep your thumbs turned down and rotated backwards. Once your arms are all the way in front of your head, just hold them there as you flutter kick until you need to breathe. Then pull your arms under your body as you take a quick sneaky breath. Repeat.

TIP: Master straight arms by doing "water angel" drills.

Once you've mastered this drill, you can begin to progress toward butterfly by changing the flutter kick to a body dolphin. Eventually modify the drill so that you are doing one angel with every pulse of body dolphin. You will find that, for most swimmers, the best timing for one-pulse-water-angels is to connect the hands to the hips so that when the hips break you can start the recovery. At this point, you should adjust your recovery so that your arms are just an inch or so over the surface of the water. By the way, if you've got this far, congratulations because this version of one pulse water angels also has another name; it's called butterfly! The thing is, don't just jump to the end drill. Spend time, a lot of time – several weeks at least, doing each drill until you absolutely master it. If you rush it, you will not see a long term improvement in your strokes.

TIP: Connect your hands to your hips. When your hips break the surface, start your recovery!

WHEN TO BREATHE

Clearly we all know how to breathe. The question in butterfly is *when* to breathe. Let's take a look at what we now know and see if we can't figure this one out. We know that when we lift our heads up, our hips will sink. If our hips sink we are going to have to use our legs and do a big kick to push back up onto the surface. That would mean that our kick isn't going to do much good in terms of moving us forward. So, we probably should try to breathe in a way that minimizes how far our hips sink and how much drag we add.

A TALE OF TWO BREATHING METHODS

If you watch people swim butterfly, you will quickly begin to see that many of them do the exact opposite. Instead of minimizing how far the hips sink, their breathing actually maximizes the sinking action. After several heats you will begin to notice a pattern. The swimmers that have the most difficulty with the stroke are lifting their heads to breathe at the start of the underwater pull and not finishing until the hands re-enter the water.

Science tells us why this is a very bad idea. We already talked about the head position above, but if you start breathing when you begin the underwater pull and keep your head up until you recover, think about where your hands are. At some point during the underwater pull they are all the way down by the hips. At that point your elbow has already passed ninety degrees and no longer has power to balance and propel the body while breathing. With your head to breathe at this moment, you cannot possibly stay balanced. As a result, you start to quickly sink; forcing you to do a very big, bent knee, kick. This causes even more excess drag and really brings the stroke to a dead stop. The simple solution if you start breathing when you begin your underwater recovery is to finish your breath by the time your elbows are at ninety degrees during your arm pull which occurs just under your chest.

TIP: Breathing just before the end of the underwater pull causes your hips to sink and may cause an extra knee bend. This adds drag and slows you down.

Balance isn't the only problem! By not finishing your breath until your hands are past your chest, the anatomy of your body works against you. In butterfly it is much more difficult to bring your arms around the surface if your head is up. Having your head up also makes it almost impossible to reach full extension. Many swimmers are creating nerve impingements in their shoulders by keeping their heads up out of the water and breathing during the recovery. This can ultimately lead to severe shoulder problems after a few years.

TIP: It is almost impossible to bring your arms around the surface and reach full extension when your head is up!

THE PERFECT BUTTERFLY BREATH

Above we discussed a quick way to improve your breathing if you prefer to start your breath as you begin your under water pull. However, because of the sine wave action your body is making there is another place to breath that will get you a slightly faster time. It does so because it allows all of your underwater pull to go into moving your body forward. When you lift your head to breath during your underwater pull, some small amount of energy is lost in balancing your body. As always, try both methods and see which feels and works best for you. Keep in mind that if you have been doing fly for a while, this new method will definitely take some time to get used to and will feel and look very weird to you.

Let's try it a different way. We will connect the breathing to your body rotation. It sounds weird, but when you think about it, it makes perfect sense! Hopefully by this point you already had a chance to try the body dolphin rotation drills. As you recall, when doing a butterfly recovery, you should connect your hands to your hips. This means that as your hips surface, your hands will just be ending the underwater pull and will surface at the same time as your hips. At this moment, you can begin the recovery. At the very next moment, just as your hands begin to move forward, your hips should start to move back down in the water. This is the proper timing for the recovery and it is the perfect place to take a breath!

Why? At this moment your hips are already, naturally, on their way down in the wave of your body dolphin. Remember, when you lift your head you are going to make your hips drop down. So, this is absolutely perfect timing! Why not lift our head at the exact moment when we actually *want* our hips to go down!? Just remember not to lift it too high out of the water or your hips will sink too far and create extra drag!

TIP: Remember not to lift your head too high out of the water during the breath. Always try to stay so low during a breath that your nose touches the water the entire time!

To make everything work perfectly, you should finish your breath and begin getting your face back to the surface at the moment your hips are deepest in the water. This should happen exactly as your arms are straight out to your sides during the recovery. If you begin your breath just as you are starting your recovery and finish as your arms are straight out to the side, then place your head back on the surface as you enter your hands in the water, you will have mastered the perfect butterfly breath! You will actually be using your breath to drive your body dolphin and increase your speed! What makes this feel odd to many swimmers is that it forces them to complete a full breath in half the time they are used to taking.

156

TIP: Time your breath to your body dolphin. Begin at the end of the underwater pull as your hips are dropping down again; end as your arms are straight out to your sides and your hips begin to surface.

A PIE IN THE FACE

One thing to avoid is face smashing. Many times swimmers don't have the breathing timed correctly face planting in the water. In some cases it will look like the swimmer is doing an extra pulse of head lead body dolphin. When breathing, you should imagine that your head is placed on top of a skateboard on the surface of the water that simply rolls forward with your body. Look down and allow your face to glide just above the surface on your imaginary skateboard.

TIP: When breathing, pretend you head is rolling along the surface on a skateboard. It should be aimed down and roll forward over the surface of the water.

When you first work on timing the breathing have a coach or a friend observe. If they report that you are face planting then you may need to adjust your timing. However, the most common reason for face planting is that the swimmer hasn't mastered breathing with body dolphin. It might be a good idea to take the arms out of the equation and do a few lengths of body dolphin with your arms at your side. First try breathing every three pulses and you will want to keep rolling through the breath. Once you've mastered that reduce to breathing every two pulses and finally breathe every pulse. Ensure that you do not stop while breathing and that your body continues to roll through each breath. Once you've got your timing, go back to the butterfly and see if the face planting is gone.

TIP: If you are face planting during breathing, take the arms out of the equation. Master breathing with body dolphin, then add the arms back.

It is vitally important to your time that you lift your head out of the water as little as possible. Finally, remember that it is *not* necessary, nor is it even a good idea to breathe every stroke in butterfly! Try doing it at a three stroke interval. You will be stunned at how much time you drop as you reduce the number of breaths you take.

TIP: Do not breathe every stroke in butterfly. Try to set a rhythm of three to five strokes per breath as you would do in other strokes.

A WORD ABOUT THE PULL

Coach X has been around for a while and he has worked with many swimmers and many coaches. Most swimmers don't even bother to ask how far back they should pull during the butterfly. This is usually because their coach has already engrained in them that they should be pulling all the way back to their hips. But is this really the best approach? Again, it is the goal of the *Super Sprinter* to ask questions about everything and when in doubt do the research. It turns out that according to science, it is *not* as efficient to pull all the way down to your suit as it is to focus on keeping your hands out in front of you in the water. That said, this would be a very good time to point out the difference between efficiency and speed.

Many coaches and swimmers often get the concepts of efficiency and speed confused. It is true that it is more efficient to keep your hands extended in front of you when swimming butterfly versus pulling your arms all the way to your suit, but it does not mean that it is faster to do so. As it turns out, you most likely will go faster by pulling all the way down to your hips.

However, doing so uses more energy and burns through your oxygen and electrolyte supply faster. There are races for which the distance makes it non practical for a swimmer to pull down all the way. At longer race distances, the speed increase is quickly outweighed by the energy drain. In general, the drag reduction you get by placing your hands in front of your body will outweigh the speed gain you may get by pulling to the suit.

How do you know which is the better choice? Actually, for most of you this is going to be pretty easy. In short races where it is very important to use every last bit of energy in your muscles and you don't care about the energy drain from distance then, most definitely, you should be pulling down to your suit! In longer races like a 200 fly, you will want to conserve some of that energy and save some of the strength in your arm muscles. In these races, it will be more effective to favor a shorter pull, keeping your arms in front of you. Keep that pattern until the end of the race. When you need that burst of speed, reach in and do a full pull. Remember you should still try to reach as far forward as possible.

TIP: It is less efficient to pull all the way to your suit in butterfly. In longer races, favor a shorter pull!

Finally, if you are having a hard time putting it all together, there is a great and fun drill that Coach X would like you to try. Get a water polo ball or any light ball and place it in the lane in front of you. As you do your butterfly, bump the ball with the top of your head, then as you recover your arms, capture the ball with the back of your wrists (don't grab it with your hands). This may take a few attempts to get used to, but when you do, your butterfly will start to look gorgeous and you will be well on your way to becoming a *Super Sprinter.*

BUTTERFLY TIP SUMMARY

GENERAL

TIP: Don't over complicate butterfly! Think of it as body dolphin with arms.

TIP: The muscles in your knees and arms are Type II, short-twitch white fibers and are not designed for long term power output. They will give out quickly if you rely on them in butterfly.

TIP: Your abs are built for long lasting power! Use them instead of your knees and arms to provide power during butterfly.

TIP: Be careful not to overdue butterfly. If you feel pain in your shoulder notify your coach immediately; it means you are doing something wrong!

BALANCE

TIP: To remain balanced in fly requires you put more pressure on your chest and face to get your hips up.

TIP: Use the rule of three: Three things must break the surface, the back of your head, your shoulders, then your hips or briefs in that order.

ROTATION

TIP: Pop your belly button to drive your hip rotation and setup an efficient body dolphin.

TIP: Drive your butterfly propulsion with your rotation, not with your arms!

TIP: The deeper you go, the longer the pool becomes and the slower your time.

PULL

TIP: Where your hands go, your body will follow. Place the hands on the surface; do not claw into the water.

TIP: The further you stretch your arms in front of your head, the less drag on your body and the faster you go!

TIP: Do not claw into the water; this will cause you to dive too deep! Keep your arms straight during a butterfly recovery.

TIP: It is less efficient to pull all the way to your suit in butterfly. In longer races, favor a shorter pull!

KICK

TIP: Never bend your knees in fly; curve your legs and allow the wave to flow from your hips out your toes!

TIP: If you are having trouble mastering body dolphin, start from a vertical body dolphin in the deep end.

TIP: If you have truly mastered body dolphin for butterfly, you should be able to body dolphin backwards almost as fast as forwards!

RECOVERY

TIP: When doing a fly recovery it is important to keep your arms low and straight.

TIP: Turn your thumbs down or backward during the recovery to lock your elbows and guarantee a straight arm recovery!

TIP: Master straight arms by doing "water angel" drills.

TIP: Connect your hands to your hips. When your hips break the surface, start your recovery!

TIP: It is almost impossible to bring your arms around the surface and reach full extension when your head is up!

BREATHING

TIP: Breathing just before the end of the underwater pull causes your hips to sink and may cause an extra knee bend. This adds drag and slows you down.

TIP: Remember not to lift your head too high out of the water during the breath. Always try to stay so low during a breath that your nose touches the water the entire time!

TIP: Time your breath to your body dolphin. Begin at the end of the underwater pull as your hips are dropping down again; end as your arms are straight out to your sides and your hips begin to surface.

TIP: When breathing, pretend you head is rolling along the surface on a skateboard. It should be aimed down and roll forward over the surface of the water.

TIP: If you are face planting during breathing, take the arms out of the equation. Master breathing with body dolphin, then add the arms back.

TIP: Do not breathe every stroke in butterfly. Try to set a rhythm of three to five strokes per breath as you would do in other strokes.

PUTTING IT ALL TOGETHER

BALROTELONPROP

Hopefully you have had an opportunity to try some of the experiments in this book. Coach X loves experiments! Over the course of the book you should have seen some common themes reoccurring for each of the four strokes. Here is a scientifically based word that you should remember: BALROTELONPROP.

This word has been scientifically designed to get stored in a different part of your brain (the hippocampus) than most words (the prefrontal cortex). In fact if you are under ten you will likely not forget this word for the rest of your life. Kind of cool, right? The reason is that in order to pronounce this word, your brain has to work in a unique way. It has to analyze the word and try to make sense of it. You will first use the rules of language that you have learned over the years, but since the word doesn't look quite like other words, you will have to guess at how it is pronounced. Coach X will give you a hand. It is pronounced:
BAL – ROT – E – LAWN – PROP.

Just as your brain had to put it all together, this word helps to put together all the ideas around the strokes. In order of scientific importance there is balance, elongation, rotation and propulsion. There is clearly a lot of additional science that goes into swimming, but it can all be categorized into these four main areas. As you go back and re-read these chapters you will undoubtedly notice this order is repeated for each stroke throughout the book.

This was no mistake. It is vitally important to your success as a *Super Sprinter* that you learn to improve your strokes in this order. Coach X strongly cautions you not to jump ahead. Far too many swimmers think they already know everything there is to know and just need to focus on one thing or the other. As a result they ignore important first steps and the results are usually not very good.

Down in El Salvador, Coach X once coached a group of Olympic trainers and athletes. You can bet that these people thought they knew how to swim and how to coach, and it was definitely rough going for the first day. Imagine a group of elite swimmers being told, "We will not be swimming at all today." You can probably imagine the looks Coach X got from the Olympic trainers. But by applying the same science described in this book, the worst improved athlete still had an eight percent improvement in efficiency and two percent in speed. By the end of the clinic, every athlete and every Olympic trainer was on board and wanted more.

There is *so* much more that Coach X wants to write and tell you, but this is after all, only a handbook. The format necessitates that I keep it short. There is so much science left untold: The science behind swimming psychology, nutrition, coaching methodology, drills, and so much more. It is Coach X's hope that you will enjoy the lessons of this book and pass along the information to your friends. Better yet, encourage them to buy a copy of the book for themselves!

Coach X said it at the beginning; everything in this book works because science says it has to work – period! There is no voodoo coaching here, no guessing, no hog wash, no "my coach said this works", no superstition. Science is the only way to get rid of all the garbage technique that's out there. By following the path of science you WILL become the *Super Sprinter* that you've always known you could become.

Throughout the book I have tried to insert as many stories from real swimmers as possible to help bring some sense of real world success to the book. Before Coach X leaves you with one last story, he wants to encourage you to share your own stories. You can leave an e-mail for Coach X at SBSCSWIM@GMAIL.COM. Tell us your name, age and story and maybe it will end up in the next *Super Sprinter* book! You can also use this email address to inquire about clinics, but we prefer you visit www.sciencebasedswiming.com. Here now at the end I leave you with one more story to inspire you to become your own *Super Sprinter:*

REVIEWER'S STORY

While writing this book, Coach X sought the help of several swimmers from around the world. He wanted to make sure that the content was useful and not too technical. You can read about this in the foreword to the book. Because this book took years to create, Coach X wanted to make sure he did a lot of quality research, we were actually able to monitor the effects the book had on those that reviewed it versus other similar level swimmers.

West coast based swimmers who reviewed the book all went on to do some amazing things. They set new team records, competed in Far Western competitions, competed in All Star teams, most competed at Nationals and two even went to Olympic trials. Coach X specifically remembers one swimmer who read an earlier version of the book that talked about why briefs were faster than jammers. This swimmer told his friends who did not believe him. When the swimmer went on to break the team records, the friends all switched to briefs and after listening to advice from the book, they too began to show huge time drops.

East coast swimmers did equally well. In fact, one swimmer is now a coach himself and has gone on to be featured for his performances in triathlons. He is able to save quite a lot of energy due to the science based swimming techniques he learned, from this book. It also turns out he's just an awesome runner and bicyclist.

One Midwest swimmer credits this book for changing his breaststroke. He actually called to say that his coach did not like the changes suggested in this book, but the swimmer insisted the new techniques were making him faster. Eventually the coach relented and allowed the boy to swim breast using the science based principles in this book. At age fifteen that boy went from an average swimmer on his team to an Olympic

Trials swimmer dropping from a 1:13.00 in the short course 100 breast to a 57.30. He will very likely make the Olympics in 2016.

Swimmers from other countries have gone on to amazing results as well. They have taken high point awards, competed at meets around the world, been selected for elite meets and travel teams. Two swimmers actually swam in the Olympic Games. They have all distinguished themselves far beyond other swimmers who started at their same ability level before they reviewed the book.

The thing that all these swimmers have in common is that they were able to take the ideas and science from this book and apply it directly to their swimming. Coaches from around the world have written and called to express their joy around seeing their mediocre swimmers become the best performing athletes on their team.

Now it is your turn! It may not happen overnight, but if you practice the science based principles of this handbook you will very quickly begin to see your times drop. You will soon see yourself rising through the ranks of your team and eventually you may even break a few records yourself. Coach X always likes feedback from swimmers who have improved from science based swimming so please share your stories.

164

EPILOG

IT'S TOO LATE BABY

There are approximately 300,000 age group swimmers in the United States and while many begin their careers as young eight and under swimmers, many do not. Several swimmers do not join the sport until well into their teenage years and many more never join at all because they believe that it is just too late for them to start. Coach X has seen this first hand many, many times and when he does, he always intervenes and tells this story:

ANONYMOUS OLYMPIAN'S STORY

As it turns out this is not the story of just one Olympic athlete, but rather of two. Neither swimmer started the sport until they were a teenager. What might surprise you is that most of their story is so similar to every other teen, and maybe even your own. The first athlete grew up in the Midwest in a very small town. It was the type of place that was an awesome place to grow up, but not the kind of place where one would expect to find an Olympic class athlete. This particular swimmer was bullied horribly during middle school and high school. Finally in his sophomore year at high school, he decided that he would try to get back at his bully in a very unique way. He discovered that his bully was the fastest swimmer on the high school team. So that year, when the team had tryouts, our friendly newbie went to the pool.

The coach asked what stroke our swimmer wanted to do for his try-out. He looked over at his bully and said to the coach, "What stroke does he do?" The coach said it was backstroke, so our swimmer said, "That's my stroke, I want to do backstroke."

It should be pointed out at this time that our hero in this story had never swam before in his life. In fact he never even had a lesson. Even more remarkable was the fact that he actually had to be rescued by a lifeguard at a beach when he stepped out past the buoy line and nearly drown when he was younger. Despite all of this, he was determined to one day swim faster than the boy who had bullied him for six years.

When he jumped in the water, he had never put on a racing suit before and thought it made him feel incredibly fast. In his first ever time trial, he swam a 100 yard backstroke in 1:12.44. Not too bad for someone who had never swam in his life! As it turned out this time was actually good enough to earn him a spot on the Varsity team for his high school. But he turned it down!

Our swimmer instead asked the coach how the bully was able to earn his way onto the varsity team. The coach said it was from his time, but that there were three other ways to earn a spot on the varsity team. One way was to earn enough points at the swimming meets during the season, the second was to beat someone who was already on varsity, and the third was to place in the top eight at the sectionals meet. Our swimmer decided that if the bully made the varsity team on time alone, that he would make varsity every way possible. The coach told him that no swimmer in the history of the school had ever done so. But our swimmer persevered! He was able to earn his varsity letter in every possible way. As it turned out he was not only the first person at his school to do this, but the first person in the entire state!

There is more you need to know about this remarkable story. Unlike so many fantastic moms and dads today, this swimmer had absolutely no support from his family. Keep in mind that this swimmer lived in a very cold climate and his high school swim team took place in the winter. He had to find his own way to and from practice each and every morning and evening. His parents did not come to any practices nor did they come to even one swimming meet. During parent's night he actually had to give the rose to his friend's mother so that he would not be embarrassed for people to see that his own parents did not come.

Despite this setback, our swimmer was able to drop his time from a 1:12:44 to under 57.3 seconds by his senior year. Eventually this swimmer went on to college where he was able to qualify for the Olympics. Rather than give any more details, Coach X will end the story here so as to not give away the swimmers identity.

Our second story is about a man who became one of the fastest breast stroke swimmers in the world. Coach X again does not want to give out too many details so as to avoid identifying the Olympic athlete, however when he was younger, he was certainly not considered a great swimmer. He often jokes that he was considered the team mascot because he was short and pudgy. It was his older brother that was the team star and was clearly going to be an Olympic athlete. But when things were looking the most positive, tragedy struck. This swimmers older brother contracted a fatal disease and passed away at a very young age.

The passing of his older brother had an incredibly strong and profound effect on this hero. Coach X simply cannot do justice to the feelings and so he won't even try. The fact of the matter is that our swimmer went through a very rough time, struck with grief. He found solace in the pool. It was his one refuge and place where he could take out his anger at the world. He would be the first one in the pool each day and the last one out. And then, it happened. He decided that if his brother could no longer make it to the Olympics, then he would do it in memory of his brother. Each and every practice our swimmer would push himself harder and harder, well beyond his normal limits. He would literally try to push himself to the point of complete exhaustion until he simply had nothing left. In a few short years after he turned fifteen, he went from being the fat chubby team mascot to being the fastest breaststroke swimmer in the entire world!

The lesson to be learned from these stories is that anyone, even someone starting the sport at age fifteen or sixteen can become an Olympic athlete! You simply need to believe in yourself and never, ever, give up!

If this is your story, then don't despair. You've picked the right book! You have no idea how many Olympic athletes around the world didn't start swimming until their high school years. It only takes desire and some science to become the next *Super Sprinter*!

Coach X would like to truly thank you for purchasing and reading this book. Even if you don't know it yet, you are a great swimmer. And, Coach X can't wait to watch you in the Olympics one day. Hang in there; you're going to be fantastic!

-    Coach X

ABOUT THE AUTHOR

Coach Kurt Schallitz has been interested in science based swimming for well over two decades. He travels around the world working with thousands of swimmers in his unique clinics that teach the science behind the strokes.

He has been fortunate enough to work with hundreds of top coaches around the globe and has used their insights to help refine stroke techniques through the lens of science. When not coaching swimming, Kurt enjoys giving speeches at local high schools on Science Technology Engineering and Mathematics.

Kurt began his swimming career when he was in high school. During this time, Kurt would often ask the coach why he was doing a given drill. Not to upset the coach, but in a genuine interest to understand the mechanics of every drill. In college, Kurt chose not to swim on the. When initially scoping out the swim team Kurt would ask the benefit of a given drill or why the team was working on a particular technique, the coach was unable to provide a valid response. Kurt felt he could train more effectively on an independent basis.

With that in mind he began to break down all of the strokes into their fundamental components. He applied his skills in science, engineering, physics and mathematics toward each stroke. By his Junior year, Kurt was swimming exclusively backstroke up to seven hours per day. One of his friends who joined the college team asked Kurt to be part of a mock meet to get an "official" time. Kurt agreed and did a 46.44 in the 100 yard backstroke.

His friends attempted to convince him to join the college team. Converted to a long course time, this result would have likely earned a medal in the prior Olympic Games. Kurt reluctantly decided to join the college team and was initiated during his first practice. The set was easy enough for most college swimmers 20x 100 fly on 1:10. Kurt was able to finish the set but began to experience some extreme problems. It turned out to be an ischemic stroke.

Fortunately the University Hospital was directly across the street from the training facility. However, it meant an end to Kurt's swimming career. Learning that he would no longer be able to swim competitively, Kurt turned his attention to coaching and began working with local YMCA swimmers and eventually began his own team clinics. Today he runs Science Based Swimming Clinics and travels the world bringing his unique science perspective to swimmers everywhere. He enjoys speaking at events and loves seeing average swimmers become elite level swimmers after changing just a few things in their stroke.